The *Painted* Kitchen

Over 60 quick and easy ways
to transform your kitchen cupboards

HENNY DONOVAN

David & Charles

A DAVID & CHARLES BOOK

First published in the UK in 2000

Copyright © 2000 Quarto Publishing plc

A catalogue record for this book is available from the British Library.

ISBN 0-7153-1138-7

QUAR.TPK

Conceived, designed and produced by
Quarto Publishing plc
The Old Brewery
6 Blundell Street
London N7 9BH

Editor Steffanie Diamond Brown
Art Editor Sally Bond
Assistant Art Director Penny Cobb
Copy Editor Claire Waite
Designer Julie Francis
Photographer Paul Forrester
Picture research Laurent Boubounelle
Indexer Dorothy Frame

Art Director Moira Clinch
Publisher Piers Spence

Manufactured in Hong Kong by Regent Publishing Services Ltd.
Printed in Singapore by Star Standard Industries (Pte) Ltd.

For David & Charles
Brunel House Newton Abbot Devon

Contents

▲ *The pairing of silver and white in a kitchen setting creates a clean, simple, contemporary look.*

The kitchen is increasingly becoming the heart of the home. No longer just a functional space where the task of cooking is performed, more and more people are treating the kitchen as a place to spend quality time with their families and friends. Because of this new status within the home, it is more important than ever before that the kitchen be decorated to suit the tastes and style of those who will use it most. This book has been written for precisely this purpose: to help you create your ideal kitchen. Whether you want to give your existing kitchen a facelift, design a kitchen from scratch or just disguise an unsightly feature, this book will help you create the look, feel and ambience of the kitchen you've always dreamed of.

Using paint is a simple and inexpensive way to produce a totally individual, customized look. From traditional to country, decorative to stylish, and contemporary to simple, virtually any effect you desire can be achieved with a little bit of paint and the right tools. Given the modern materials available today, the versatility of paint and the knowledge of how to use both to produce beautiful effects, a little time and effort is all you need to achieve exactly the style and finish you want.

Introduction

This book has also been written in response to the ever-increasing demand for paint effects that use water-based paints, glazes and varnishes. Water-based paints and glazes are preferable to oil-based ones for many reasons: they are safer to use, easier to clean up, emit fewer odours and are faster-drying. Further, they do not yellow, offer strength and durability and do not pollute the atmosphere with noxious chemicals.

The first section of the book concentrates on methods of preparation and finishing, and provides guidance on choosing colours. Before you get started on any of the projects, we show you how to determine what material your doors are made from, and then how to prepare them for the fabulous paint effects to follow. The tools, brushes and basic equipment you will need to create the featured paint effects are also detailed. Because it is important to understand the uses and properties of paints, varnishes and mediums, we have included a chart which provides this information, as well as coverage calculations to help you plan how much paint you will need. There is also a section on how to determine which paint effects can be applied to your particular cupboard doors (given the material they are made from) as well as which ones will most flatter their shape and style. A step-by-step guide to some of the most basic paint techniques – colourwashing, distressing and various glazing effects – is also provided. Information on how to add panelling to flat doors is included as well, along with a guide to painting door furniture and restoring original pieces. Finally, we show you how to protect your painted doors so they will stay looking beautiful for a long time.

Colour can be a baffling science, and so an introduction to the nature of colour and its use in the context of interior decoration is provided. The basics of colour theory are covered, from tone and intensity to opposite and complementary colour combinations, so you can mix your own colours knowledgeably and successfully. The difference between warm and cool colours and their impact on colour schemes and mood is also explained, to help you plan the right colour palette to achieve the effect you want.

Organized by colour, the second section of the book consists of 16 projects designed to teach you how to create some of the most stunning paint effects available today. Subtle relief-stencilled effects, innovations on traditional decoupage, polished plaster finishes, contemporary decorative scripts, vinegar glazing, modern woodgrain effects and metallic finishes are only a few of the wonderful techniques covered. Simple step-by-step instructions – accompanied by colour photographs of virtually every step – show you how to achieve each effect with ease.

▲ *The soft bloom of a limed finish adds a sense of classic distinction to open-grained hardwood doors.*

For additional inspiration, photographs of alternative cupboard door designs are integrated throughout the chapters. Each photograph is accompanied by a simple explanation of how to imitate the design, cross-referencing the techniques taught within the book, so you can learn how to create these gorgeous designs yourself.

A hands-on introduction to the world of paint effects, this book will teach you how to create your own individual look, both simply and economically. With a little practice under your belt and the techniques and ideas in this book as your guide, you will be amazed at how easy it is to transform the busiest room in the house into a place you will love spending time in.

◀ *Traditional cupboard doors can be transformed into chic, stylish kitchen furnishings with this woven denim effect.*

Preparation &*finishing techniques*

PROFESSIONAL PAINTERS AND DECORATORS know that preparation accounts for 80 percent of the success of any decorating project. This is no less true when working on a feature as prominently visible as kitchen cupboards. Without thorough preparation, the decorative finish may not bond to the surface and can lift, peel or scratch. Similarly, decorative finishes must be sealed and protected to withstand the wear and tear of the kitchen environment, which includes heavy use, regular cleaning and frequent changes in heat and humidity. Plan sufficient drying time for priming and base coating, and for sealing and varnishing. The more time left between coats, the more durable the decorated surface will be.

Preparation

The preparation of your doors will be determined by their surface and the finish already on them. Ideal surfaces for painting are bare and untreated, but in many cases you will have to deal with existing paint, stains, varnish, wax or polish, or manufactured surfaces such as melamine or vinyl. Decide whether the doors need to be stripped back to their original surface, or require just simple sanding for a smooth finish. Check that the quality of the doors warrants the work, and that they can withstand the different treatments; doors that are either rickety, warped or coming apart at the joins are not good subjects for decorative finishes, unless the finish is intended as a temporary facelift until new doors can be fitted.

The method of preparation required will also depend on the finish already on the doors. If you are unsure whether they were finished with an acrylic or oil-based product, treat them as if finished with an oil-based product. Finally, it will be easier to work on your doors if you remove them from their cupboards first.

DOOR COMPOSITION

WOOD
Solid wood: Solid wooden doors are most commonly made from pine or oak, but can also be made from mahogany, ash, maple or birch.

Laminate: Laminate doors consist of layers of compressed wood compounds such as MDF or chipboard sandwiched between layers of wood such as pine, mahogany or birch.

Veneer: Similar to laminates, veneers comprise a thin layer of high-quality wood stuck to a solid wood base of lesser quality.

MDF
Made of compressed wood fibres, these doors are manufactured primarily for flat-painting, but are perfectly suitable for many other paint finishes as well.

PLASTIC
Most man-made doors consist of some sort of plastic coating attached to a chipboard or MDF base. Melamine and vinyl are the most common types of plastic used, and are produced either plain or patterned, to emulate woodgrains.

PREPARATION REQUIREMENTS

Surface	Method of preparation	Materials and tools
NEW, BARE WOOD *(solid wood or laminate)*	Sand and apply knotting solution. Apply two coats of acrylic primer.	Medium- and fine-grade sandpaper; varnish brush; knotting solution; natural bristle paintbrush; acrylic primer
WATER-BASED PAINTS ON WOOD *(solid wood or laminate)*	Clean, sand and prime with acrylic primer. Where many layers of paint have been built up, use a commercial paint stripper. Sand and prime after stripping.	Diluted detergent; cloth; medium- and fine-grade sandpaper; natural bristle paintbrush; acrylic primer; gloves; goggles; commercial paint stripper; paint scraper
OIL-BASED PAINTS ON WOOD *(solid wood or laminate)*	Clean. Scrape off or strip uneven, flaking or blistered paint. Sand down and fill any cracks with wood filler. Sand well and prime with acrylic primer or acrylic convertor.	Diluted detergent; cloth; metal paint scraper; gloves, goggles; old paintbrush; commercial paint stripper, coarse- and medium-grade sandpaper; putty knife; wood filler; natural bristle paintbrush; acrylic primer or acrylic convertor
WATER-BASED STAINS ON WOOD *(solid wood or laminate)*	Clean, sand, and prime with acrylic primer.	Diluted detergent; cloth; medium- and fine-grade sandpaper; natural bristle paintbrush; acrylic primer
OIL-BASED STAINS ON WOOD *(solid wood or laminate)*	Remove stain with wire wool and white spirit. Clean, sand, and prime with acrylic primer or acrylic convertor.	Medium-grade wire wool; white spirit; medium- and fine-grade sandpaper; natural bristle paintbrush; acrylic primer or acrylic convertor
WATER-BASED VARNISH ON WOOD *(solid wood or laminate)*	Clean, sand and prime with acrylic primer.	Diluted detergent; cloth; medium- and fine-grade sandpaper; natural bristle paintbrush; acrylic primer
OIL-BASED VARNISH ON WOOD *(solid wood or laminate)*	Clean. Scrape off or strip uneven, flaking or blistered paintwork. Sand and fill any cracks with wood filler. Sand and prime with acrylic primer or acrylic convertor.	Diluted detergent; cloth; paint scraper; gloves; goggles; old paintbrush; commercial paint stripper; coarse- and medium-grade sandpaper; putty knife; wood filler; natural bristle paintbrush; acrylic primer or acrylic convertor
CELLULOSE VARNISH ON WOOD *(solid wood or laminate)*	Sand with wet-and-dry sandpaper until smooth. Seal with white polish shellac and prime with acrylic primer.	Coarse- and medium-grade wet-and-dry sandpaper; varnish brush; white shellac; natural bristle paintbrush; acrylic primer
SHELLAC/LACQUER/ FRENCH POLISH ON WOOD *(solid wood or laminate)*	Remove polish with methylated spirits and wire wool, then neutralize with hot water and detergent. Sand and prime with acrylic primer.	Medium-grade wire wool; methylated spirits; detergent; cloth; medium-grade sandpaper; natural bristle paintbrush; acrylic primer
WAX ON WOOD *(solid wood or laminate)*	Remove wax with methylated spirits and wire wool, then neutralize with hot water and detergent. Sand, then prime with acrylic primer.	Medium-grade wire wool; methylated spirits; detergent; cloth; medium-grade sandpaper; natural bristle paintbrush; acrylic primer
WOOD VENEER	Veneer should be fully secured, not peeling or torn. Sand carefully and prime with acrylic primer.	Fine-grade sandpaper; natural bristle paintbrush; acrylic primer
BARE, NEW MDF	Sand, then coat with watered-down PVA glue (1 part glue to 3 parts water). Apply acrylic primer. Make sure all edges are sealed.	Medium- and fine-grade sandpaper; two natural bristle paintbrushes; PVA glue; acrylic primer
WATER-BASED PAINTS ON MDF	Clean, sand and prime with acrylic primer.	Diluted detergent; cloth; medium- and fine-grade sandpaper; natural bristle paintbrush; acrylic primer
OIL-BASED PAINTS ON MDF	Clean, sand and prime with acrylic primer or acrylic convertor.	Diluted detergent; cloth; coarse- and medium-grade sandpaper; natural bristle paintbrush; acrylic primer or acrylic convertor
MELAMINE, FORMICA AND VINYL	Clean with hot water and detergent. Sand with wet-and-dry sandpaper, then apply two coats of acrylic melamine primer or acrylic convertor. Do not sand between coats.	Detergent; cloth; medium-grade wet-and-dry sandpaper; synthetic paintbrush; acrylic melamine primer or acrylic convertor
WATER- OR OIL-BASED PAINTS ON MELAMINE, FORMICA OR VINYL	Apply commercial paint stripper and scrape off paint. Clean with detergent, sand with wet-and-dry sandpaper and prime with acrylic melamine primer or acrylic convertor. Chipped, flaking surfaces are unsuitable for repainting.	Gloves; goggles; old paintbrush; commercial paint stripper; metal paint scraper; diluted detergent; cloth; medium-grade wet-and-dry sandpaper; synthetic paintbrush; acrylic melamine primer or acrylic convertor

Preparation techniques

Planning enough time for preparation is just as important as allowing time for your chosen decorative technique. Although the preparation stage can be less than exciting, it is essential that it is done properly. Every moment spent preparing your doors will reap huge rewards in the long run, while skimping on this process can diminish the results – or even lead to having to redo the work.

CLEANING

Ensure that the surface is clean and free of grease and loose particles. Use household detergent diluted in water or sugar soap (follow package instructions) and wipe down with a clean cloth. Avoid saturating the surface. Doors covered with thick grime will need the stronger solution of sugar soap, which must be washed off after use.

STRIPPING

Layers of thick, uneven paint and varnish cannot be rubbed back with sandpaper alone; a commercial paint stripper is needed. Strip cupboard doors by hand, since professional dipping may cause warping or force the joins to come undone. Wear protective gloves and goggles and follow the manufacturer's instructions. Strippers are most effective when they are applied liberally and left to soak for at least 30 minutes. Remove softened paint using a metal paint scraper.

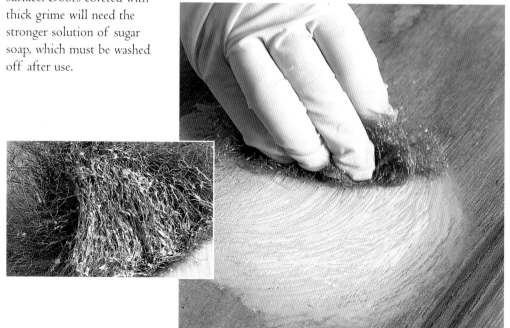

REMOVING STAINS, WAXES AND POLISHES

Water-based paints will not adhere to surfaces that have previously been stained with oil-based stains, or waxed or polished. Remove oil-based stains using medium-grade wire wool and white spirit; waxes, polishes and shellacs can be removed using medium-grade wire wool and methylated spirits. Wipe down with diluted detergent. When dry, sand thoroughly.

SANDING

Sanding has many uses: it removes old paint, loose materials and varnishes; creates a smooth working surface and a key; smoothes surfaces after stripping or wire wool treatments; and smoothes wooden doors between coats of primer, emulsion and varnish. Choose coarse, medium or fine grades in either glass or wet-and-dry sandpaper, depending on the smoothness required (see page 7). Sand wood in the direction of the grain; MDF, melamine and vinyl should be sanded straight up and down. Wear a face mask to avoid dust inhalation.

FILLING AND SEALING WOOD

Using a putty knife, apply wood filler to wooden doors with sections of grain missing or cracks in the moulding. Allow to dry, then sand. Do not use resin-based fillers if you are using an acrylic primer. For paint finishes that require a smooth surface, doors with a very open grain will also need filling – fine filler designed for walls can be used for this purpose. Seal knots on new, bare wooden doors by applying knotting solution with a paintbrush. This will prevent resin from the knots seeping through to the final paint finish.

PRIMING

When the surface is smooth, apply a coat of primer (see page 7 for primer type). If the base coat to follow is a strong colour, tint the primer with a universal tinter for easier coverage. Primers seal the surface, provide initial coverage and create a bond between the surface and the paint. For panelled doors, apply primer to the inner panel first, starting with the moulding. Then apply liberally to the rest of the inner panel using a criss-cross motion; lay off by brushing up and down. To prime the outer panels or frame, first apply horizontally to the top and bottom, then vertically to the sides. For flat doors, apply primer liberally using a criss-cross motion; lay off by brushing up and down.

APPLYING THE BASE COAT

Once the door has been primed, apply one or two coats of base colour – either water-based highly pigmented wood paint or emulsion – using a decorators' paintbrush. Apply the paint in the same way as priming, brushing it on in a criss-cross motion and laying off by brushing up and down for a smooth finish. On wooden and MDF doors, sand between coats with fine-grade sandpaper. Do not sand between coats on melamine, man-made laminates or vinyl surfaces; apply the paint on these surfaces as evenly as possible.

Paints, brushes *&useful equipment*

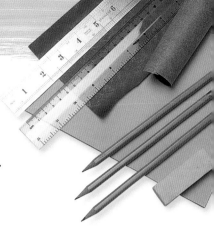

Before beginning your project, determine which equipment and materials you will need to produce the paint effect. It is important to have everything on hand, as some finishes will require you to work quickly.

USEFUL EQUIPMENT

You will find much of the general equipment used to produce paint effects around the home or in the toolbox. Other items may warrant a trip to the DIY shop.

Dust sheets protect the surrounding areas from paint or solvent spills.
A **dust mask** is useful when sanding, as the fine dust produced can irritate your nose and mouth.
Sandpaper and wet-and-dry paper comes in fine, medium and coarse grades.

Wire wool is available in different grades: fine, medium and coarse.
A **firm wire brush** is used to rake out the grain of hard woods before liming.
A small, **soft wire brush** is used to remove liming paste.
Use a **decorators' sponge** to wipe down surfaces and to apply colourwash.
General-purpose **cotton cloths** are used to clean the surface in preparation, as well as for scumble glaze effects such as rag-rolling.

Protective gloves should be worn when using paint strippers. You may also wish to wear them when working with paints and glazes if your skin is easily irritated.
A **paint kettle** is necessary for mixing paints and glazes.
A **mini roller** is used for inking up stamps.
Use a **mixing palette**, such as a plastic tub, an old plate or a clean foil container, for mixing small amounts of paint.
Candle wax from a plain white household candle is used to create a wax resist in distressing techniques.
Low-tack spray adhesive can be used to temporarily stick stencils and other designs to surfaces.

Low-tack masking tape is used to mask off areas you do not wish to paint.
Use **low-tack lining tape** to mask off areas when painting straight lines.
Teaspoons (tsp) and **tablespoons (tbsp)** are used when measuring out paints, glazes and plaster.
Rags and **lint-free polishing cloths** are used to apply and buff waxes.
A **spirit level** helps mark an accurate horizontal line, and is useful when working on doors that are still attached to cupboards.
Use a **tape measure** when planning measurements over a large area.

Firm wire brush

Mini roller

Spoon

Paint kettle

Mixing palette

Dust mask

Soft wire brush

Wire wool

Low-tack spray adhesive

Sandpaper

Decorators' sponge

Protective gloves

Cotton cloths

Dust sheets

Candle wax

Plastic & metal rulers, pencils, drawing rubber, transtrace & tracing papers

Use a 45 or 30cm (18 or 12 in) **plastic ruler** for marking up guidelines.
A 30cm (12 in) **metal ruler** is helpful when scoring designs into wood using a scalpel.
Use a sharp **scalpel** to cut stencil designs and score into wood.
It helps to have good-quality, sharp **scissors** when cutting out decoupage motifs and metal transfer leaf.
Have a variety of **pencils** on hand for marking up guidelines and designs.
A **drawing rubber** will remove pencil marks once a decoration has dried.
Transtrace and **tracing paper** are used to transfer drawn or photocopied designs onto a surface.
Have photocopy, laser or layout paper on hand for sketches, designs and layouts, and for keeping track of measurements.

Lint-free cloth

Scalpel

Tape measure

Scissors

Spirit level

Low-tack masking & lining tape

PAINTS, VARNISHES AND SPECIALIST MEDIUMS

Paint is made up of three main ingredients: pigment, binder and a medium or vehicle. The pigment provides colour and covering power; the binder, which hardens as it dries, causes adhesion to the surface; and the medium makes application possible. There are three main paint families: water-based, oil-based, and methylated spirit- or alcohol-based. Solvents are used to dissolve the paint and make cleaning possible. The solvent for water-based paint is water; for oil-based paint use white spirit or turpentine; and for methylated spirit- or alcohol-based paint use methylated spirits. Most of the products used in this book are water-based, with the exception of shellac, wax and polyurethane varnish. Water-based products are preferable in that they are non-toxic, virtually odourless and environmentally safe (they must be disposed of in accordance with local waste regulations, however). This chart highlights some of the products available for painting, staining, varnishing, waxing and creating special effects.

Product	Water-based varieties	Oil-based varieties	Alcohol-based varieties
PRIMERS AND DECORATING PAINTS FOR FURNITURE AND WOODWORK	Acrylic primer Acrylic convertor Melamine primer Acrylic eggshell Emulsion High pigment paint (undiluted) Stencil paint	Oil undercoat Eggshell paint Gloss paint Enamel/Japan paint	Cellulose paint
ARTISTS' PAINTS FOR APPLIED DECORATION AND TINTING	Artists' acrylic paint Gouache Universal tinter	Artists' oil paint Oil pastel	
SPECIALIST EFFECTS AND FINISHES	Acrylic glaze Colourwash Impasto, polished plaster Combing paste Liming paste Crackle glaze Craquelure varnish	Oil-based glaze Linseed oil	White polish shellac Button polish shellac French polish
BINDERS FOR SPECIALIST FINISHES	PVA glue Rabbit-skin glue Acrylic gilding size	Japan gilding size	
STAINS	Highly pigmented wood paint (diluted) Water-based stains and dyes Universal tinter	Oil-based stains	
WAXES		Coloured wax Beeswax Paraffin wax Carnauba wax Liming wax	
VARNISHES AND SEALERS	Matt acrylic varnish Eggshell acrylic varnish Gloss acrylic varnish Metallic acrylic varnish	Flat oil-based varnish Eggshell oil-based varnish Gloss oil-based varnish Polyurethane varnish Yacht varnish	Knotting solution Shellac

BRUSHES AND THEIR USES

Brush	Used for	Technique
25 and 50mm (1 and 2 in) natural bristle paintbrushes	Priming, applying emulsion and wood paint, and general usage.	Load a liberal amount of paint onto the tip of the brush. Paint using criss-cross strokes or straight strokes.
25 and 50mm (1 and 2 in) synthetic paintbrushes	Priming and painting onto man-made surfaces; good for most acrylic paints.	Load a liberal amount of paint onto the tip of the brush. Paint using criss-cross strokes or straight strokes.
25 and 50mm (1 and 2 in) varnish brushes	Applying varnishes and shellacs.	Do not overload the brush. Glide the brush over the surface using light, smooth strokes.
Fitch brush	Mixing paints, painting panels and mouldings, and painting small areas and edges.	Use the tip of the brush to work the paint.
Artists' sable brush	Hand-painting and detail, and applying gilding size to small areas.	Keep the paint on the tip of the brush for optimum control. For loose strokes, as in a folk-art style, hold the brush in the middle of the handle. For more controlled work, hold the brush nearer to the base of the bristles.
6 and 13mm (¼ and ½ in) sable or nylon one-stroke brushes	Hand-painting, applying washes to small areas and mouldings; good for creating clean edges.	For washes, hold the brush in the middle of the handle and load liberally with paint. For more detailed work, hold the handle nearer to the base of the bristles and use less paint.
Stencil brush	Stencilling, stippling; good for fine spattering.	When stencilling, always choose a large brush. Control the brush by placing an elastic band around the base of the bristles. Always use a dry brush and as little paint as possible when stencilling.
Hog-hair softener	Softening and blending colourwash effects (apply colourwash with decorators' sponge first); can also be used for stippling and for moving glaze as it becomes sticky.	Hold the brush handle nearer to the base of the bristles and use soft, long, sweeping criss-cross movements.
Stippling block	Stippling glaze and textured effects in thick paint.	Used in a 'pouncing' motion, either for its own effect or for evening out glazes before dragging or combing. Dab the block at right angles to the surface.
Dragging brush	Dragging through glaze.	Drag the brush down through the glaze, or towards you if working flat. Repeat this action in downward stripes until complete. Some areas may need going over again for an even dragged effect.
Flogging brush	Wood graining and some marble effects; can also be used for dragging.	Starting at the bottom of the glazed area, hit the surface in a flogging action with the flat tip of the brush moving upwards, or away from you if working flat. Repeat from bottom to top until complete.
Pencil overgrainer	Woodgraining and some marble finishes.	Pull the overgrainer down through the glaze in a swerving motion – the degree of waviness will depend on the desired grain effect.
Badger-hair softener	Woodgraining and marbling; used to soften the marks created by a previous brush.	Lightly brush over the marks already made in the same and opposite directions.
Rubber decorating comb	Combing glaze and textured paints.	For straight lines, comb towards you or downwards. For wavy lines or other effects, comb freestyle.
Decorators' steel float	Application and smoothing of polished plaster work such as Venetian plaster, marmorino and stucco.	Take up some plaster onto the float and smooth over the surface in an arcing movement. Repeat action to remove any excess plaster and ridges.

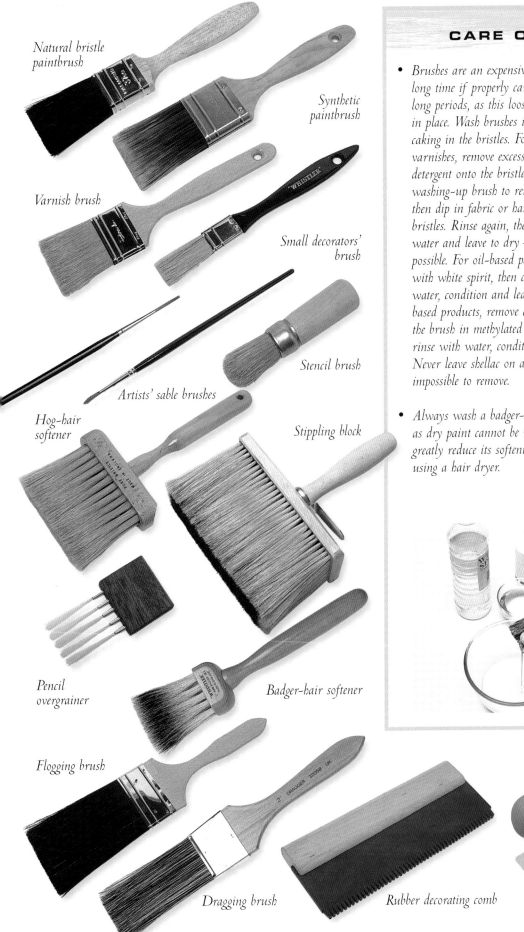

Natural bristle paintbrush

Synthetic paintbrush

Varnish brush

Small decorators' brush

Artists' sable brushes

Stencil brush

Hog-hair softener

Stippling block

Pencil overgrainer

Badger-hair softener

Flogging brush

Dragging brush

Rubber decorating comb

Decorators' steel float

CARE OF BRUSHES

- Brushes are an expensive investment, but will last for a long time if properly cared for. Do not soak brushes for long periods, as this loosens the glue that holds the bristles in place. Wash brushes immediately after use to avoid paint caking in the bristles. For water-based paints and varnishes, remove excess paint with water, then put some detergent onto the bristles and work through with a nail or washing-up brush to remove all traces of paint. Rinse, then dip in fabric or hair conditioner to condition the bristles. Rinse again, then squeeze out. Shake off excess water and leave to dry – flat initially and then hanging, if possible. For oil-based paints and varnishes, rinse first with white spirit, then clean with detergent, rinse with water, condition and leave to dry, as above. For alcohol-based products, remove all traces of the product by dousing the brush in methylated spirits. Clean with detergent, then rinse with water, condition and leave to dry, as above. Never leave shellac on a brush; once it hardens, it is impossible to remove.

- Always wash a badger-hair softener immediately after use, as dry paint cannot be removed from the brush and will greatly reduce its softening ability. The brush can be dried using a hair dryer.

UNIVERSAL TINTER GUIDELINES

Universal tinters or stainers are highly concentrated colouring agents. Care should always be taken when using them, especially as some colours are stronger than others. The strength of the colour obtained will depend upon the medium being tinted and the amount of white within that medium. It is important to note that tinters have no binder and no drying power of their own, so if you wish to use them for hand-painting, they must be mixed with a medium that has a built-in binder, such as a varnish, glaze or artists' acrylics. The following chart is offered as a guideline for strength and usage, and roughly reflects the amount of medium that can be used for two doors. As a general rule, add the tinter a drop or two at a time, monitoring the results as you go. Amounts will vary between brands, so always check the manufacturer's instructions before use, and test for varying strengths.

Colour	Medium	Pastel shade	Mid-tone	Full colour	Medium	Pastel shade	Mid-tone	Full colour
RAW UMBER, BURNT UMBER	Acrylic glaze	2 drops	5 drops	10-15 drops	White emulsion and polished plaster	5-10 drops	20-30 drops	50-60 drops
RED IRON OXIDE, RED, BURNT SIENNA	Acrylic glaze	1 drop	3 drops	6-8 drops	White emulsion and polished plaster	3 drops	6-8 drops	15-20 drops
YELLOW OCHRE, YELLOW	Acrylic glaze	3 drops	6-8 drops	15-20 drops	White emulsion and polished plaster	10 drops	30 drops	50-60 drops
GREEN, BLUE, PURPLE	Acrylic glaze	2 drops	5 drops	10-15 drops	White emulsion and polished plaster	5-10 drops	20-30 drops	50-60 drops
WHITE	Acrylic glaze	2 drops	5 drops	10-15 drops	White emulsion and polished plaster	10 drops	30 drops	60 drops

HEALTH AND SAFETY

- *Be sure to read and follow the manufacturer's instructions carefully on all products.*

- *Always work in a well-ventilated area.*

- *Wear protective rubber gloves to avoid direct skin contact when using oil- and alcohol-based products.*

- *When using water-based products, avoid lengthy exposure to the skin to prevent irritation or drying out. Wear protective gloves if you have sensitive skin.*

WHAT DO THE PRODUCTS DO?

This chart provides a brief description of the main paints and materials used in this book and explains what they are used for. There is also a coverage calculation reference, to help you plan how much of each product you will need.

Paints and materials	Product description
ACRYLIC PRIMER Coverage: 1L up to 12m² (2 pints up to 36 ft²)	A water-based primer for sealing and covering wood and MDF surfaces.
MELAMINE PRIMER OR ACRYLIC CONVERTOR Coverage: 1L up to 12m² (2 pints up to 36 ft²)	A water-based primer for sealing and covering melamine, vinyl and other man-made surfaces. Can also be painted over oil-based paints (after sanding) as a base for water-based paints.
EMULSION Coverage: 1L up to 10m² (2 pints up to 30 ft²)	A water-based paint designed for use on walls, but can be used for most furniture as well. Available in matt (flat) and silk (mid-sheen) finishes.
WOOD PAINT Coverage: 1L undiluted up to 12m² (2 pints up to 36 ft²)	A matt, opaque, undiluted paint specially formulated for wood. Contains a built-in primer, and has a high chalk and pigment content. It covers well and is of better quality than emulsion. Ideal for high-quality flat-painting, distressing, burnishing and stencilling. Can also be diluted with water to create a wash for bare wood. Should not be confused with colourwash.
STENCIL PAINT Approximate coverage: 4.5L up to 500m² (1 gallon up to 1500 ft²)	Specialist water-based paint formulated for stencilling and stamping. Good for hand-painting.
ARTISTS' ACRYLIC PAINT Coverage: A good squeeze will tint 500ml (1 pint) by one shade	Good for hand-painting. They can also be used for tinting acrylic glazes or paints, but must be diluted first to guarantee proper colour dispersion. Not as strong or cheap as universal tinters, but possess good adhesive properties.
ACRYLIC SCUMBLE GLAZE Coverage: 1L up to 16m² (2 pints up to 48 ft²), although varies according to dilution	Water-based, transparent, colourless glaze. Tint to required colour with universal tinters or artists' acrylic paints. Used for many paint effects, including combing, stippling, woodgraining and marbling. A drying retardant such as glycol may be added to slow drying time. Dries to a satin finish. Seal and protect with acrylic varnish.
COLOURWASH Coverage: 1L up to 30m² (2 pints up to 90 ft²)	Specially formulated, water-based, translucent, coloured glaze containing glycol retardants. Also available clear for tinting. If not available ready-made, can be created by mixing three parts acrylic scumble glaze (preferably matt) with one part water to the consistency of single cream. Can be tinted using universal tinter. Creates a soft bloom of colour with a satin, matt finish. Seal with acrylic varnish in areas subject to wear and tear.

Paints and materials	Product description
UNIVERSAL TINTERS Coverage: see tinter chart, left	Versatile, water-based tinting agent. Highly concentrated liquid colour that disperses well in all products. Can be used to colour thick paints, plaster finishes, limewash, distemper, glazes, acrylic varnish, shellac and oil-based paints. Unsuitable for use with cellulose-based mediums.
IMPASTO OR TEXTURED PAINT Coverage: 1L up to 4m² (2 pints up to 12 ft²)	Thick paint designed for textured effects on walls, but equally effective on furniture as a relief-stencilling medium. Can be coloured with universal tinters, or colourwashed.
POLISHED PLASTER/VENETIAN PLASTER/MARMORINO Coverage: 1kg up to 1m² (3 lb up to 3 ft²)	Specialist plaster finish for distressed and polished effects. The plaster contains lime and marble dust, and can be polished with a decorators' steel float for a smooth finish. Colour with universal tinters or dry pigments (need to be dissolved first). Beautiful when colourwashed.
LIMING PASTE Coverage: 1L up to 16m² (2 pints up to 48 ft²)	Thick, chalky, water-based paste applied to hardwoods with an open grain. Remove with a soft wire brush once dry for a silvery bloom. Seal with white polish shellac and acrylic varnish.
CRACKLE GLAZE Coverage: 1L up to 16m² (2 pints up to 48 ft²)	When applied between two layers of water-based paint, this water-based medium causes the top coat of paint to crack and open up, revealing the colour underneath.
CRAQUELURE VARNISH Coverage: 1L up to 16m² (2 pints up to 48 ft²)	A water-based, two-step cracking varnish that produces an antiqued effect over painted surfaces and decoupage. The top coat varnish is applied over the dry base coat varnish. As the top coat dries, cracks appear due to a reaction between the two layers. Artists' oil paint or coloured wax is rubbed into the cracks for emphasis.
ACRYLIC GILDING SIZE Approximate coverage: 60ml up to 1m² (4 tbsp up to 3 ft²)	Water-based glue used to adhere metal leaf and metallic powders.
ACRYLIC VARNISH Coverage: 1L up to 16m² (2 pints up to 48 ft²)	Water-based varnish available in matt, eggshell or gloss finishes. Non-yellowing and quick-drying.
SHELLAC Approximate coverage: 1L up to 8m² (2 pints up to 24 ft²)	Alcohol-based, fast-drying lacquer. White and button polish shellacs are used to seal many decorative finishes. Enables the transfer of work between oil- and water-based mediums. Does not replace varnish and requires a protective coat.

Door types

K itchen cupboard doors are made from a variety of materials with a range of finishes. A basic ability to identify which material a door is made from is necessary in order to ascertain its suitability for a particular paint finish.

The materials from which kitchen cupboard doors are made typically fall into two categories: wooden and man-made. Both categories of materials appear in many forms, however, and it can be difficult to tell the two types apart: solid woods can resemble laminates, and man-made materials often imitate woods. An examination of the door's joints may help reveal its true nature: wooden doors, unless they are a single carved piece, have genuine joints, such as 'dovetailed' joints, clearly visible at the top and bottom edges; all laminates, whether natural or plastic, have visible (if only faintly) seams on their inside edges; and man-made doors that emulate wood usually have no joints at all.

The categories 'wooden' and 'man-made' can be broken down even further. Wooden cupboard doors can be made from solid wood, laminate or veneer; MDF doors are made from compressed wood fibres; and plastic doors are typically made from melamine or vinyl attached to an MDF or chipboard base (see page 6 for further detail).

▼ *Featured from far left to right*: Solid oak door, made from bare, untreated wood; solid pine door, made from untreated, knotty pine; melamine affixed to an MDF base; cherry wood vinyl wrapped onto a shaped chipboard base.

SUITABILITY OF SURFACES

Wooden surfaces are almost always the most suitable base for paint finishes. This is because paint bonds well to wood, thereby increasing the life span of the finish and enhancing its beauty. Paint finishes on wooden surfaces are also less prone to cracking and chipping. Finishes suitable for wooden surfaces include flat-painting, distressing, liming, faux marquetry, leaf stippling, impasto relief stencilling, colourwashing, combing, vinegar glaze effects, scumble glaze effects, craquelure, crackle glaze, stencilling, stamping and hand-painting. Polished plaster and stucco effects work best on MDF surfaces.

Good results can be obtained on melamine and vinyl surfaces as well, as long as plenty of drying time is allowed (for each layer to fully cure and bond). The application of a paint finish to a plastic surface is recommended as a temporary measure only; it is not a long-term solution. The paint effects that work best on melamine and vinyl surfaces are those that do not involve thickly textured paints and plasters, and do not require the type of vigorous working which might cause the underlying coats of paint to peel away. Suitable finishes for use on these surfaces include flat-painting, colourwashing, dry-brush work, stencilling, stamping, hand-painting, decoupage, checks and woodgraining (the latter two effects will need extra drying time).

Countertops and work surfaces should not be embellished with paint effects, since they receive too much wear and tear. A very simple effect, such as stencilling or stamping, could be added to solid wooden worktops, but only if protected with several coats of yacht varnish.

Do not attempt extensive paint treatments on doors that are chipped, or on doors where the laminate is coming away from the base, as the paint may bubble and scratch and will not last.

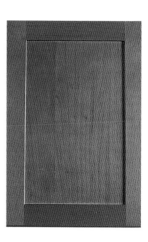

Matching door styles
with paint effects

There are many different styles of kitchen cupboard doors: flat, tongue-and-groove, Shaker-style, classic panelled country-style, modern, with a small inner panel and a wide frame, and traditional, with a raised central panel and an arched top, are some well-known examples. Contemporary door styles tend to show simple lines and very little detail, while many traditional doors have detailed panelling and frames. While most paint finishes are versatile enough to be adapted to suit a multitude of different door styles, certain finishes are better suited to some styles than others. As a general rule, flat doors or doors with wide Shaker-style frames are best for more modern, contemporary designs, such as those achieved using polished plaster or metallic paints. Doors with moulding or panelling are very well-suited to more traditional paint effects, such as distressing; they also work well in conjunction with elaborate finishes, notably those in which hand-painted detail covers only a section of the door. An example of each type of finish – modern, traditional and elaborate – is shown below, having been applied to the particular door style that flatters it most.

▲ Polished plaster finishes work especially well on plain, flat surfaces, such as this MDF door. The flatness of the surface makes the application of the plaster easier, and complements the modern look created by this technique.

▲ Panelled or tongue-and-groove doors are well suited to distressed finishes, for which the moulding or detail acts as the worn edge. Here the distressing is light enough so as not to dominate the overall look, yet it is visible enough to highlight the moulding and hand-painted script.

▲ A raised inner panel and moulding can act as a natural frame for a pretty hand-painted motif, such as this folk-art design.

Choosing a technique

When deciding on a paint effect, think about the look you're after. The colour scheme and door style will both be relevant factors to consider. After choosing a paint effect and colour scheme, practise the technique and try mixing the colours before painting on the actual door. Below is an overview of some of the most commonly used techniques.

DISTRESSING

This technique requires some patience because of the many layers of paint involved, but it will last a long time. Examples of distressing can be seen on pages 34-37, 87, 102, 103, and 105. Prime the door (see pages 6-9) and apply two coats of highly pigmented wood paint or matt emulsion using criss-cross movements, and laying off with vertical strokes. Smooth with fine-grade sandpaper.

1 Rub a household candle onto areas most likely to wear, such as mouldings and corners, and onto some flat areas. Do not cover the whole door. Go back over the same areas to ensure a build-up of wax.

2 Apply one or two coats of highly pigmented wood paint or matt emulsion (depending on the strength of the base colour) in a second colour. The paint may become bumpy as it reacts with the wax. Leave to dry.

3 Use medium-grade wire wool or sandpaper to lightly rub paint back from the waxed areas, revealing the base coat beneath. If the wire wool produces grey marks, these can be removed with soapy water. Keep the distressing subtle for a realistic look. Finish by sanding over the whole door with fine-grade sandpaper to create a burnished, smooth surface. Seal with two coats of matt acrylic varnish.

COLOURWASHING

In this technique, the base paint shows through the top coat to reveal soft, broken colour. Examples of colourwashing can be seen on pages 43, 72-75, 85, and 104. Work on one door at a time. After priming (see pages 6-9), apply two even coats of base colour using the same technique as for distressing. Use either non-absorbent matt emulsion or ordinary matt emulsion sealed with matt acrylic varnish. Leave to dry for a minimum of 24 hours, then apply the colourwash, as below. If ready-made colourwash is unavailable, mix three parts acrylic scumble glaze and one part water to the consistency of single cream. Tint with universal tinter to the desired shade (see tinter guidelines, page 14), and apply as below.

1 Pour approximately 15ml (1 tbsp) of colourwash onto a decorators' sponge.

2 Wipe the colourwash onto the door surface in swirling figure-of-eight movements, until the whole door is covered. Make sure that there are no gaps in the colourwash.

3 Brush over the colourwash with a hog-hair softener immediately, using light criss-cross movements to soften the effect. Work swiftly, before the colourwash becomes tacky. Allow to dry for 24 hours, then apply a coat of matt acrylic varnish. Decorate further if desired, then finish with two coats of matt acrylic varnish.

SCUMBLE GLAZE EFFECTS

These effects should always be applied on non-absorbent surfaces painted with either vinyl silk paint, acrylic eggshell paint or a paint varnished with an acrylic eggshell varnish. Always allow 24 hours for the paint effect to harden, then finish with three coats of matt or eggshell acrylic varnish.

Here we look at some scumble glaze effects that work well on cupboard doors. The same glaze is used for each effect, but the tools and techniques used to make patterns on the wet glaze differ. Examples of scumble glaze effects can be seen on pages 52-55, 121 (combing); 90-93, 105 (dragging); 44, 85, 94-97, 122 (spattering); and 45, 108-111 (rag-rolling).

DRAGGING

Use a small dragging brush for panelled doors and a full-size brush for flat surfaces. Drag through the glaze for an even effect.

COMBING

Both rubber and steel combs with different sized teeth are available. Use either to create straight lines, checks, circles or swirls.

STIPPLING

'Pounce' a stippling block firmly up and down onto the glaze, holding the block at a right-angle to the surface, until the texture is consistent. Remove excess glaze from the block as you go.

SPONGING

Dampen a sea sponge and squeeze out any excess water. Lightly bounce the sponge over the glaze, creating a soft, mottled texture. Subtle colour combinations (close in tone or tint) work best.

1 Mix two-thirds acrylic scumble glaze with the final third made of equal parts matt acrylic varnish and water. Colour with universal tinter if desired (see guidelines, page 14). Here we have used four drops of burnt sienna and two drops of raw umber tinter. Stir well. If painting doors, mix a bit of matt acrylic varnish into the glaze to speed up drying time and for durability (do not add varnish if painting walls, as a longer drying time is required).

2 Use a 25mm (1 in) paint- or varnish brush to apply the glaze to the whole surface. Brush out the glaze in criss-cross movements, then even out using vertical strokes. You will need about 15ml (1 tbsp) of glaze for an average-sized door. After the glaze has been laid on and before it dries, the desired technique can be applied. Changes will be hard to make once the glaze becomes sticky, but while still wet you can wipe it off completely with a damp cloth and start again.

RAG-ROLLING

Dampen a lint-free cloth. Scrunch into a ball, then twist into a 'sausage' shape. Start at the bottom and roll the cloth upwards in an arc. Repeat over the entire door.

SPATTERING

Dip a stencil brush into the glaze, shaking off any excess. Flick the brush down over your finger. Repeat over the entire door (be sure to protect surrounding areas).

Door furniture

Door furniture has become a fashionable interior accessory in its own right, with countless styles and finishes on the market to choose from. Junk shops are always worth a trawl for old handles or knobs that can be restored, and plain wooden knobs can be bought and painted to match or contrast with the paint effect on the door.

PLAIN WOODEN KNOBS

Virtually all of the techniques in this book can be applied to a plain wooden door knob. A few simple options designed to complement a wide range of different door decorations are illustrated here. If you decide to paint your knobs to match your doors exactly, do so at the same time as you paint your doors to avoid having to remix colours or glazes.

COLOURWASHING AND WAXING

Prime the knob (see pages 6-9) and apply a base coat, then colourwash to match the door's decoration (see Colourwashing, page 18). For further depth of colour and extra sheen, try applying an antiquing or coloured wax. Buff with a clean cloth.

CRAQUELURE

Base coat the knob with an ivory matt emulsion or high-pigment wood paint. Shellac, then apply both steps of the craquelure varnish. When dry, rub raw umber artists' oil paint into the cracks and buff with a cloth. Allow to dry for 24 hours. Apply a coat of shellac and then matt polyurethane varnish or eggshell acrylic varnish.

METALLIC COATING

This medium is available through specialist artists' outlets. Apply the coating to the knob following the manufacturer's instructions, and allow to harden for 24 hours. Rub with medium-grade wire wool to reveal the sheen, then burnish with the back of a spoon to create extra shine.

RESTORING ORIGINAL PIECES

If your door furniture is made of brass, it may be tarnished or covered with lacquer or paint. To remove tarnish, soak in household vinegar overnight, then rub back with wire wool. Finish with a commercial brass cleaner. To remove lacquer, use a lacquer thinner, following the manufacturer's instructions. Add one part methylated spirits to four parts lacquer thinner to speed up the process. Rub back with wire wool. To remove paint, use a commercial paint stripper following the manufacturer's instructions. Use wire wool to remove any stubborn bits of paint. Always wear protective gloves and work in a well-ventilated area when using chemicals.

Turning flat doors *into panelled doors*

A plain, flat door can be livened up considerably by the addition of a frame of beading or moulding. These embellishments can also be useful if you wish to use a paint finish that requires raised areas on the door, such as distressed finishes, hand-painted detail that benefits from a frame or finishes that are only applied to one section of the door, such as craquelure or crackle glazing.

A range of different kinds of beading and moulding are available at good timber merchants, where you can have the pieces custom cut and mitred (diagonally cut). Give the timber merchant the inside measurements of the four lengths that comprise the rectangular frame.

3 Place the four lengths of 45-degree mitred wood on the glue. Make sure all the corners are at 90-degree angles – use a set-square or triangle to check. Press down firmly.

4 Use 25mm (1 in) tacks (smaller for beading that has less depth) to hammer through the beading to fully secure it to the door surface. Use up to three tacks on the longer lengths and two on the shorter ones. If there are any gaps in the joints, fill using a commercial wood filler (following the manufacturer's instructions). Leave to dry for 24 hours, then sand as necessary.

1 Using a pencil and ruler, draw a rectangle onto the door that matches the size of your beading strips. Make sure the rectangle is aligned 'square' to the door.

2 Apply undiluted PVA glue to the marked area; alternatively, apply the glue to the back of the beading. Leave for about five minutes, or until the glue is tacky.

Finishing *techniques*

Care taken in finishing your doors is particularly important in the kitchen, which receives some of the heaviest wear and tear in a house. The doors must be carefully sealed and protected with varnish so they can be wiped down regularly and will stay looking good.

TYPES OF FINISHES

With its shiny, varnish-like finish, shellac can be used as a sealer, but it is not strong enough to be used on its own as a protector; it must be finished with varnish as well.

Water-based acrylic varnishes are easy to use as well as durable. They are also preferable because they do not discolour over time, as all oil-based varnishes do. Most of the projects in this book are finished with acrylic varnishes for this reason, with the occasional use of oil-based polyurethane varnish, where an ageing, yellowing look is actually desired.

Waxes provide a water-resistant finish only; they are not waterproof, and thus are not generally suitable for the kitchen (although they are fine on overhead cupboards). Coloured wax can, however, be used sparingly over a prevarnished surface on small sections of a door, as the varnish will enable the surface to be wiped down. Water splashes will mark a waxed surface over time, so do not use wax near sink areas.

HEALTH AND SAFETY

- *Always read and follow the manufacturer's instructions on all products, and work in a well-ventilated area.*

- *When using oil- and alcohol-based products, wear protective rubber gloves to avoid direct skin contact.*

- *When using water-based products, avoid lengthy exposure to the skin. Wear protective gloves if your skin is sensitive.*

- *Dispose of all leftover products and soiled rags according to the manufacturer's instructions and local regulations.*

SHELLAC

Shellac is used for sealing gilded and decoupaged effects, and on paint finishes for a lacquer-style finish before varnishing. White polish shellac is bleached, so it won't discolour the finish it is applied to. Button polish shellac is honey-coloured, and is perfect for achieving an instant antiqued look. If button polish is unavailable, tint white polish with burnt sienna, raw umber and yellow ochre universal tinters for a similar look. The solvent in shellac (methylated spirits) evaporates rapidly, so careful application is required. Dip a varnish brush into the shellac and glide it onto the surface. After laying on, brush through only twice before evaporation starts, or the smooth look will be spoiled. A single coat should take 15-20 minutes to dry. Wait two hours before applying a top coat of varnish.

ACRYLIC VARNISH

A water-based varnish, acrylic varnish is available in matt, eggshell and gloss finishes. Paint effects with a chalky, matt look, such as colourwashing, are best protected with matt varnish. Eggshell and gloss varnishes are better for gilding and dark colours, as these styles suit a reflective surface, and because matt varnish can result in a milky look. Using a varnish brush, apply an even coat of varnish over the surface, brushing it out to avoid ridges. The white sheen will disappear once dry. Apply a minimum of two coats.

POLYURETHANE AND URALKYD VARNISH

Polyurethane varnish is an inexpensive and easy-to-use oil-based varnish. It is available in matt, eggshell and gloss finishes. With exposure to light, oxidation will occur, causing yellowing. This varnish is recoatable within six hours and has a strong, durable finish. Uralkyd varnishes contain a UV filter to combat yellowing, so they are clearer than plain polyurethane varnishes. These varnishes are also strong and durable. Using a varnish brush, apply an even coat of varnish over the surface, brushing it out thoroughly to avoid unevenness. Sand lightly with fine-grade sandpaper between coats, removing dust with a cloth slightly dampened with white spirit.

SPECIALIST AND METALLIC VARNISHES

Modern advances have led to the development of water-based metallic finishes, thereby extending the range of varnishing options available. These metallic varnishes can be purchased at specialist outlets, and come in pearlescent, graphite, gold, silver and copper finishes. They are recoatable after one hour, and are best applied over prepainted surfaces. Use a varnish brush to evenly lay on the varnish. Lay off in one direction only; the direction of the brush affects the way the varnish reflects light, so brush upwards or downwards (but not both), or you will end up with a striped effect. Work quickly, as these varnishes are quick-drying. Apply a second coat for extra depth of colour or for a stronger metallic effect.

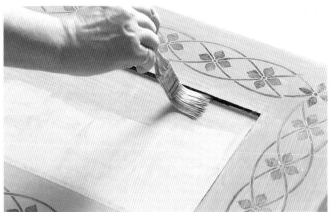

COLOURED WAX AND GILDING WAX

Both waxes are generally used to highlight mouldings or panelling. They are best applied after one or two coats of acrylic varnish. Using a lint-free cloth, apply coloured wax to the desired area. Wait five minutes, then buff. Using a lint-free cloth or a sable paintbush, apply gilding wax to the desired area. Leave as is, or buff. Do not use wax near sink areas.

LIQUID WAXES

Liquid waxes are available from specialist outlets and are easy to use. Use them only on doors that will not be subject to a lot of moisture or will not need repeated cleaning. Brush on the wax using a varnish brush. Leave for about 20 minutes, then buff with a lint-free cloth.

Choosing *colours*

The most important colour decision for any room in the house is which colour to paint the walls. The kitchen is the exception to this rule: cupboard doors are the most prominent surface space in this room, and thus their colour will define its mood. The walls are also an important feature, however, and so it is important to coordinate their colour scheme with that of the cupboard doors. You may decide to go for softer, broken colour on the walls – a colourwash, perhaps – and a bright splash of solid colour on the doors; or, conversely, you may prefer a subtle, distressed finish on the doors and simple, flat-painted walls.

The next few pages provide all the information you need to make the right colour decisions, from colour basics and mixing to using colour to create a desired mood. Some important advice: give yourself plenty of planning time, get to know the unique features of your kitchen and experiment with various colour palettes by mixing up samples before making your final decision.

UNDERSTANDING COLOUR BASICS

Understanding a few basics about colour and the theory behind it is all you really need to get started; the rest is up to your imagination, and is all about having the confidence to experiment.

Beyond the basics, the choice of colour is subjective; it is all about what works best for you. Try out different colour combinations on sheets of paper and hold them up to your cupboard doors or the walls in your kitchen to help you visualize how they will look. When you find something you like, test it out by painting a small section of the door or wall; if it grabs you, go with it. Remember, if you make a mistake on the walls, the colour can be changed fairly easily – it is the doors you need to be completely sure about!

PRIMARY, SECONDARY AND TERTIARY COLOURS

Primary colours are those that cannot be created by mixing together any other colour; in other words, they are the colours from which all other colours derive. There are three primary colours: red, blue and yellow. Secondary colours are made by mixing two primary colours together: yellow and blue make green, yellow and red make orange, and red and blue make purple. Tertiary colours are made by mixing primaries and secondaries together, creating a range of browns, greys, 'dirty' purples and greens – even black can be made in this way.

WARM AND COOL COLOURS

All colours can be either warm or cool. It is easy to see where each colour lies on the colour wheel, where the predominantly warm and cool sides are apparent. It gets a bit more complicated, however, as warm and cool versions of the same colour exist on either side of the spectrum. For instance, there are both warm and cool blues, reds and yellows. This fact has implications for the mixing of paint, glaze and tinter colours in the context of decorative painting. For instance, when a warm red such as vermilion is mixed with a warm blue such as cerulean, the result is a chocolatey brown; whereas when a cool red such as alizarin crimson is mixed with a cool blue such as ultramarine or cobalt, the result is a deep violet.

The illustrations to the right show the three primary colours in both their warm and cool incarnations. Together, these six pigments provide a comprehensive palette from which any colour in the spectrum can be created.

Warm red • *Vermilion*

Cool red • *Alizarin crimson*

Warm yellow • *Cadmium yellow*

Cool yellow • *Lemon yellow*

Cool blue • *Ultramarine or Cobalt*

Warm blue • *Cerulean*

The Colour Wheel

OPPOSITE OR COMPLEMENTARY COLOURS

An understanding of the principle of opposite or complementary colours is important when choosing colours for a room. The opposite colour of each primary colour is the secondary colour sitting opposite it on the colour wheel. Thus, the opposite of red is green, of blue is orange and of yellow is purple. The pairing of opposite colours in a colour scheme can provide a welcome colour contrast.

Mixing equal proportions of opposite colours will create a range of browns and greys; adding just a bit of the opposite colour will tone down or 'dirty' a colour.

WHITE

White is considered to be the absence of colour, as it reflects all light. In a room scheme it is highly reflective, lightening dark areas and making small areas seem larger. It also lends itself to virtually all colour schemes, and can be used as part of any style of decoration. In terms of mood, off-white is easier to live with than brilliant white, which has a blue tint and thus a chilly edge.

As might be expected, white is one of the most widely used pigments, instantly adding opacity to colours (most of which have a high degree of translucency), thereby increasing its coverage ability. Adding white to a colour will also instantly cool it down. Further, the more white that is added to a colour, the more evident its pastel tones will become.

EARTH COLOURS

Earth colours were the first pigments discovered by mankind. Literally hewn from the ground, they were mixed with water and dabbed onto the walls of early cave dwellings. Today, raw umber, burnt umber, raw sienna, burnt sienna, red iron oxide and yellow ochre are the most common earth colours used, although a multitude of variations is available.

Earth colours have both warm and cold elements. Raw umber, for example, is the cooler version of the two umbers. Always keep some raw umber, burnt sienna and yellow ochre on hand when mixing glazes and tinting paints, as these colours are uniquely useful for ageing, 'dirtying', toning down and warming up all colours.

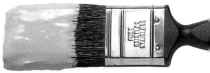

Raw Umber

Burnt Umber

Raw Sienna

Burnt Sienna

Red Iron Oxide

Yellow Ochre

METALLICS

Metallic pigments are made from ground metals, which account for their lustre and reflective qualities. All metallic paint has a certain amount of metallic pigment in it – the more pigment, the better the quality and coverage – so expect to pay more for these paints (it is worth buying the best quality you can afford). A range of metallic varnishes and paints is now available in silvers, golds and coppers, as well as pearlescent and graphite. These paints are not designed to mix with other colours, and are best applied in their own right, in sections or over appropriate bases. As metallic paints have a translucent nature, always use a base colour that takes into account – and will enhance – the metallic finish. For example, pearlescent metallic varnish is beautiful over cool pastel blues and greens; silver works well over cool greys; and gold looks wonderful over warm, sandy tones.

USING COLOUR TO CREATE MOOD

The use of colour can significantly affect the mood of a space. Certain colour combinations can make a room feel cosy and friendly, while others will give it a cooler feel. The basic rules on using colour to create mood are detailed below.

COLOUR AND LIGHT

The amount of light in a room will affect your choice of colour. In general, lighter, brighter colours reflect light, while darker colours absorb it. Bear this fact in mind when deciding whether to use dark or light colours in your colour scheme, and consider it as well in relation to the size of your kitchen. Remember also that the finish – gloss or matt – will also affect the degree of light reflection or absorption.

▲ *This soft blue colourwash effect is significantly enlivened by the complementary warm orange tones of both the wicker basket and the wood revealed through the cupboard doors.*

▲ *In this kitchen setting, warm egg-yolk yellows are paired with cool, chalky greens, demonstrating how warm and cool colours can be used together for a beautiful effect.*

WARM AND COOL COLOURS

The use of warm and cool colours will dramatically affect the mood of a room. Generally, warmer colours will seem to fill a space, giving it a more closed-in feeling, whereas cooler colours will open a space up, creating a lighter, airier environment. This does not mean that warm colours should be avoided in small spaces and cool colours in large spaces; the decision depends entirely on the mood you wish to create. You may want a small kitchen to be a cosy hub of activity and thus fill it with warm reds and terracottas, or you may wish to enhance a spacious kitchen by using pale greens and off-whites.

COMPLEMENTARY COLOURS

The impact of any colour can be increased dramatically by introducing the use of its complementary colour, even if only in small quantities as an accent. For example, if orange is put next to blue, both colours will seem more pronounced: the orange will appear more orange and the blue will look bluer. Thus, in a kitchen which has been painted predominantly blue, orange or light wooden door knobs and mouldings – and rows of cheery orange ceramic mugs and plates – would bring both colours alive.

An understanding of complementary colours can also be employed to bring out the latent undertones of a colour. For example, brown has both latent green and red undertones (it is comprised of a mix of these two colours). Thus, the placement of green next to brown will bring out the red undertones; conversely, placing red next to brown will bring out the green undertones. In this way, complementary colours can be used to enhance one another.

THE LANGUAGE OF COLOUR

Each colour has its own levels of lightness, darkness, intensity and opacity. A colour can also be affected by the medium and method used to apply it. Here we demystify the language of colour, to help you gain a better understanding of its elements.

TONE

Tone refers to the scale of light and dark in a colour. Every colour, or hue, has a range of tones. This is most easily seen on the scale of black to grey to white, yet all colours have this scale of relative lightness and darkness. If two colours have dissimilar tonal values, a sharp contrast can be seen between them; the tonal contrast between white and black shows this starkly. Tonal variations form the basis of monochromatic and contrasting colour schemes.

INTENSITY

A colour's intensity refers to its saturation. The idea of intensity is the basis for both broken-colour work and washes. Instead of lightening a colour using white, it can be diluted to become a wash. If a wash of blue is added over white, for example, the blue will remain intense and vibrant, but the overall effect created will have a paler tone due to the white showing through. All colours can be lightened or darkened by altering the base colour.

MEDIA

The type of medium used will affect the nature and character of a colour, because it will alter the amount of light absorbed or given off by the finish. For example, a glossy, shiny painted surface will reflect light, allowing a solid black to be used without fear of creating too heavy or oppressive an effect. In contrast, a gloss varnish applied over a colourwash will result in the light bouncing off the effect, thereby obscuring its depth and luminosity. Flat, chalky colours – which are matt – will absorb light. Silk finishes or polishes give off a soft sheen that is perfect for bringing out the warm undertones in wood.

COLOUR SCHEMES AND PALETTES

Students of interior design are often asked to create a 'mood board', a collage of inspirational, interesting objects and colours gathered from anywhere and everywhere and then used to work towards a coherent colour scheme. A collage based on this prototype will serve as an excellent tool to help you develop a colour scheme for your kitchen. If you are unsure of which colours to use, give yourself a few days to collect colour swatches, scraps of material, sweet wrappers, wrapping paper, old photos, pages from magazines, and so on. Even a look at the clothing you buy, your linens and other such personal purchases will reveal your preferences. Gather these items together to create your own 'still life' to get a sense of how your preferred colours work together. Continue to discard from or add to your creation until you have decided on a colour scheme. Generally speaking, kitchens call for simple colour schemes – three 'main' colours at the most is suggested. Feel free to use more than three colours, however, if they are tied together within a pattern.

▼ *Sleek, polished chrome and high-gloss granite are combined with flat grey walls and matt blue cupboards here for a clean, simple, modern look.*

Naturals & Off-whites

Naturals and off-whites increase the feeling of space, and introduce a light, airy feel. This palette ranges from the palest ivories and creams to deeper beiges, taupes and sandstones. It is important to use colours that are of a similar hue, but that have different tones, to avoid any possible colour clashes. Cream and soft coffee shades are complementary, and create a peaceful mood and a contemporary style, while pale buff and sandstone shades lend a warm, country-style feel. When using naturals in larger spaces, add accents of contrasting or deeper colours, such as warm mochas, browns, or even black, to prevent the scheme from appearing too bland. Natural fibres and textures are inherently suited to this palette — wood flooring or sisal and coir matting, bamboo and wooden blinds and wicker baskets and drawers work especially well within this colour scheme.

Relief impasto *stencilling*

A NEW TAKE on the well-known use of stencils, raised relief work is an impressively chic, yet simple way to bring modern textured finishes into everyday surroundings. This effect can be used to imitate intricate carvings or mouldings, adding style and elegance to flat or plain surfaces. It can also introduce a uniform theme into a kitchen with cupboard doors of different shapes and sizes.

Impasto, a thick, textured paint that produces a raised finish, and is relatively quick-drying, is used here. It can be painted, colourwashed and sanded back to create a subtle, distressed look. Used in conjunction with metallic effects such as metal leaf or gilt creams, it can lend a lavish, sumptuous feel to a kitchen. Or, as shown here, it can be applied using a neutral colour scheme for a simple, modern style.

MATERIALS AND EQUIPMENT

ACRYLIC PRIMER
CREAM MATT EMULSION PAINT
IMPASTO PAINT, OR A THICK TEXTURED PAINT
PALE GREY COLOURWASH
2 DECORATORS' PAINTBRUSHES
VARNISH BRUSH
HOG-HAIR SOFTENER
DECORATORS' SPONGE
SHEET OF PAPER
BORDER OR LINEAR STENCIL
METAL RULER
PENCIL
LOW-TACK SPRAY ADHESIVE
OLD CREDIT CARD OR DECORATORS' STEEL FLOAT
FINE-GRADE SANDPAPER
MEDIUM-GRADE SANDPAPER
MATT ACRYLIC VARNISH

1 • PREPARATION

This technique is suitable for solid wooden or MDF doors, but is unsuitable for melamine, vinyl or laminate surfaces. Prepare the door following the instructions on pages 6-9, applying two coats of acrylic primer. Apply a coat of cream matt emulsion. When dry, sand using fine-grade sandpaper.

2 • MARKING UP

Choose a border or a linear stencil. On a panelled door, draw marks along the centre of the outer panel with a pencil; on a plain door, the marks should be about 40-50mm (1½-2 in) in from the edge. Make the same marks at intervals all around the door. Join the marks together to create a registration guide, to be lined up with the centre of the stencil design.

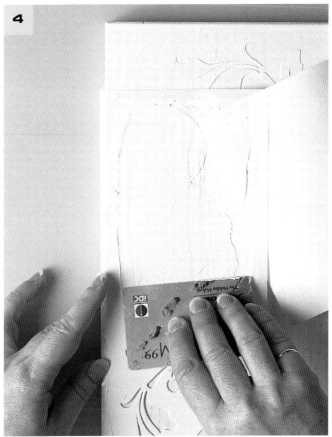

3 • STENCILLING WITH IMPASTO

Decide how often you will need to repeat the stencil design, and at what intervals. Start stencilling in the middle of each length of the door. Spray the back of the stencil with low-tack spray adhesive, line it up with the registration guide, and affix it firmly to the door. Spoon 10ml (2 tsp) of impasto or a thick textured paint onto the edge of a credit card or a decorators' steel float. Pull the card lightly over the stencil at a 45-degree angle until the stencil is covered evenly. Gently peel away the stencil without disturbing the pattern created. Allow each stencil repeat to dry fully before stencilling the next.

4 • MITRING CORNERS

Mitre each corner by positioning a sheet of paper at a 45-degree angle underneath the stencil – this will create a professional-looking, picture-frame corner. Allow each corner section to dry before stencilling the adjacent corner.

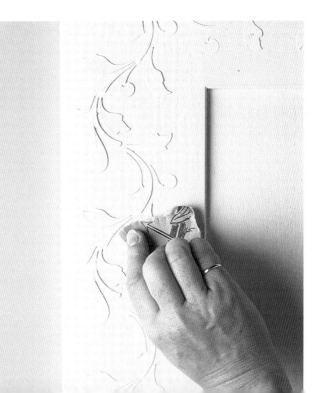

5 • SANDING ROUGH EDGES

When the stencilled sections are completely dry (up to two hours), lightly sand back any rough edges using fine-grade sandpaper. Brush or vacuum away excess dust.

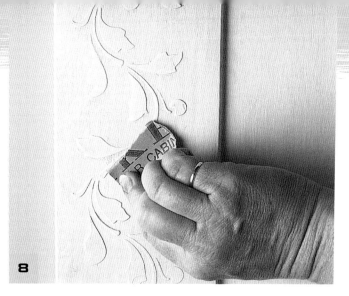

6 • OVERPAINTING

Apply a fine, even coat of cream matt emulsion over the entire door, taking care to brush out any excess paint that has gathered around the relief stencil design. Do not 'overload' the paintbrush, or the fine detail of the relief motifs may be lost. Allow to dry thoroughly.

7 • COLOURWASHING

Using a varnish brush, apply a coat of matt acrylic varnish all over. This will create a non-absorbent base for the colourwash. Let the varnish dry thoroughly. Pour 15ml (1 tbsp) of pale grey colourwash onto a decorators' sponge, then spread over the door's surface using swirling movements. While the colourwash is still wet, lightly brush over it with a hog-hair softener in cross-hatching strokes to obtain a bloom of colour.

8 • SANDING

When the colourwash is thoroughly dry, lightly sand the raised areas using medium-grade sandpaper. This will create a distressed effect, and will reveal the paler colour of the impasto or thick textured paint underneath the colourwash. Do not oversand, or the raised areas may be flattened.

TRADE SECRETS

- *If you make a mistake while the impasto or thick textured paint is still wet, simply wipe it away with a decorators' sponge. If you discover a mistake once the impasto has dried, just sand it down and try again.*

9 • FINISHING

Apply three coats of matt acrylic varnish, allowing each coat to dry thoroughly before applying the next. We use matt varnish here to enhance the natural chalkiness of this paint technique. The relief effect will be diminished if a gloss or eggshell varnish is used, as these make textured surfaces appear flattened and uniform.

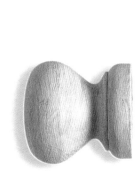

FURNITURE

Plain white ceramic or painted and colourwashed knobs are a stylishly understated choice here.

Distressed paintwork
& hand-painted script

DECORATIVE LETTERING is an increasingly popular design element in modern and contemporary interiors. With a little time and patience, everyday items can be transformed into objects with real impact and lasting beauty using decorative scripts, which blend harmoniously with today's interiors and have a timeless appeal. The ready availability of photocopiers, transfer paper and sophisticated computer fonts means you don't need to be a budding calligrapher or an artist to achieve stunning effects. The subtle distressed paint finish shown here forms a stylish, simple base for a delicate calligraphic script – all in neutral, blending tones.

1 • PREPARATION AND BASE COAT

The distressing technique is suitable for solid wood or MDF doors, but unsuitable for melamine, vinyl or laminate surfaces. Prepare the surface following the instructions on pages 6-9. Load a decorators' paintbrush liberally with smokey-brown wood paint, and spread it over the surface in criss-cross strokes, then lay off the paint by brushing back over the surface again, using upward and downward strokes to ensure a smooth, even coverage.

2 • APPLYING THE WAX RESIST

Distressing creates the natural look of a surface gently worn by the passing of time. For maximum effect, concentrate on those areas where wear and tear is most likely to have occurred. Rub a household candle along the door's mouldings, corners and edges, and also onto some of its flat areas, ensuring a good build-up of wax. Once applied, the wax acts as a 'resist', allowing the top layer of paint to be rubbed back to reveal the original colour underneath.

MATERIALS AND EQUIPMENT

SMOKEY-BROWN HIGHLY PIGMENTED WOOD PAINT

IVORY HIGHLY PIGMENTED WOOD PAINT

GOLD STENCIL PAINT OR ARTISTS' ACRYLIC PAINT

2 DECORATORS' PAINTBRUSHES

VARNISH BRUSH

FINE AND MEDIUM ARTISTS' SABLE BRUSHES

PAINT MIXING PALETTE

HOUSEHOLD CANDLE

PHOTOCOPIED SCRIPTS

LOW-TACK SPRAY ADHESIVE

PAPER SHEETS CUT TO SIZE OF DOOR

TRANSTRACE OR TRANSFER PAPER CUT TO SIZE OF DOOR

SHARP, HARD PENCIL

PLASTIC DRAWING RUBBER

MEDIUM-GRADE SANDPAPER

FINE-GRADE SANDPAPER

MATT OR SEMI-GLOSS ACRYLIC VARNISH

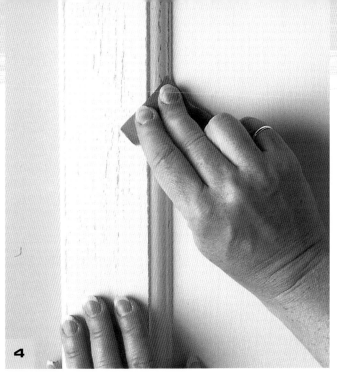

4 • DISTRESSING THE FINISH

Use medium-grade sandpaper to rub back the areas where the candle wax was applied to reveal the base coat beneath. Once all the wax has been removed and the desired effect has been achieved, rub the entire door down with fine-grade sandpaper. This will eliminate any bumps and will leave a smooth working surface for the next stage, the hand-painting.

3 • APPLYING THE TOP COAT

Using smooth, even strokes, apply two or three coats of ivory wood paint to the door, allowing it to dry between coats. Several coats will be needed because the top coat colour is lighter than the base coat. The paint may become a little bumpy over the waxed areas; this will be sanded back when the distressing is done.

5 • DESIGNING AND LAYING OUT THE DECORATIVE SCRIPT

Choose the text and style of decorative script that best suits your kitchen. In this example, a calligraphy script from a computer font has been used to style some familiar Italian and French words on a food theme. The text has then been printed out at three different sizes; or you can print out at one size and enlarge or reduce on a photocopier. Cut out your selection of words and, using a low-tack spray adhesive, stick them in the desired order onto a sheet of paper the same size as the door, to create a paper template.

6

8

6 • TRANSFERRING THE DESIGN TO THE DOOR

Lay a sheet of transtrace paper on the door. Remove one word at a time from your paper template and lay it on top of the transtrace paper, in the same position on the door as it occupies on your template. Using a sharp, hard pencil, carefully draw around the outline of each letter. The paper will transfer the design to the door, creating an outline ready for painting. Repeat with each word.

7 • PAINTING THE SCRIPT

The best effect is achieved by using colours that are similar in tone: strongly contrasting colours will make the script appear to leap off the door. Mix the two wood paint colours to create a pale beige-brown and a cream. Using artists' sable brushes, paint the largest words in beige-brown, the medium-sized words in cream and the smallest words in gold artists' acrylic or stencil paint. Leave to dry.

7

8 • FINISHING

Use a plastic drawing rubber to remove any lines or marks left by the transtrace paper or pencil. Brush away the dust. Use a varnish brush to apply a coat of matt acrylic varnish over the entire door. Take care not to overwork the varnish in case it lifts the decorative script. When completely dry, apply two more coats, for extra protection. An eggshell acrylic varnish can be used if a semi-sheen finish is preferred.

TRADE SECRETS

- *When transferring the design to the door, work from the top left to bottom right if you are right-handed, or from the top right to bottom left if you are left-handed. This reduces the chance of smudging the transferred design.*

- *Mix the paint for the lettering to the consistency of single cream. This will make application easier, and ensure good coverage.*

FURNITURE

The design is complemented perfectly by simple wooden knobs that have been given a distressed finish, as described above.

Victorian cookbook-style *decoupage*

Decoupage — the art of decorating surfaces with paper cutouts — has long been used to embellish screens and small pieces of furniture, and was a particular favourite among Victorian ladies who spent many a happy afternoon decoupaging objects as keepsakes. Here we adapt the craft, aptly using motifs from the renowned Mrs. Beeton's Book of Household Management, applied in a modern collage to create a design suitable for the kitchen. An easy and inexpensive technique, decoupage is an effective way to add interest and charm to any kitchen.

MATERIALS AND EQUIPMENT

IVORY MATT EMULSION
WHITE UNIVERSAL TINTER
DECORATORS' PAINTBRUSH
3 VARNISH BRUSHES
2 FITCH BRUSHES
PHOTOCOPIED MOTIFS
IVORY TISSUE PAPER
NEWSPAPER
SCISSORS
PVA GLUE
FINE-GRADE SANDPAPER (FOR A WOODEN OR MDF DOOR)
WHITE POLISH SHELLAC
BUTTON POLISH SHELLAC
MATT ACRYLIC VARNISH

1 • PREPARATION

Prepare a solid wood, MDF, vinyl, melamine or laminate surface following the instructions on pages 6-9. Apply two coats of ivory matt emulsion, letting the first coat dry before applying the second. Sand between coats using fine-grade sandpaper on wooden and MDF doors. Choose a selection of motifs from a decoupage sourcebook or a favourite recipe book; wrapping paper decorated with a food theme will work equally well. Make colour photocopies of the motifs you wish to use.

2 • APPLYING SHELLAC TO THE MOTIFS

Lay the photocopied motifs on newspaper. Use a varnish brush to paint a coat of white polish shellac over them, brushing it on in even strokes. The shellac seals the images, making them easy to cut and tear. Prepare plenty of motifs in this way, so you will have a good selection to choose from for your design. Allow to dry fully.

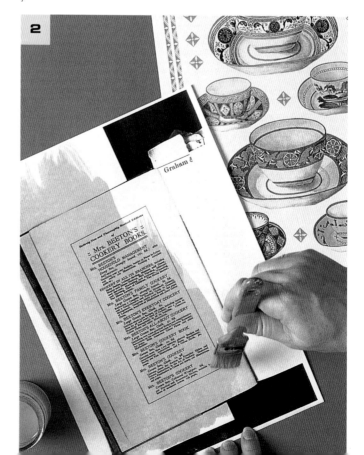

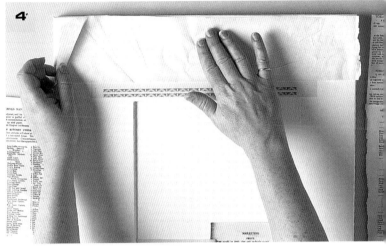

4 • STICKING DOWN THE TISSUE PAPER

Add a little water to some PVA glue until it is the consistency of single cream – if the glue is too runny, the paper will wrinkle as it dries. Paint the diluted glue onto the door with a fitch brush, then smooth the tissue paper into place with your fingertips. The tissue paper will naturally wrinkle in places; press the wrinkles down to add texture.

3 • LAYING OUT THE COLLAGE

Tear some strips of ivory tissue paper – these will act as an underlayer to the collage – and put aside. Cut out those sections or details of the motifs that you wish to use; tear others, for a different effect. Lay the motifs on the door, moving them around until you find an arrangement you like. Lay the pieces of the final design aside in the desired order, so they will be easily transferable, in this order, for gluing.

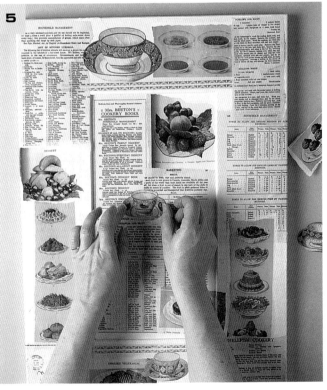

5 • STICKING DOWN THE COLLAGE

Working on one section of the door at a time, apply PVA glue to the back of each motif with the fitch brush, and press them firmly onto the door with your fingertips. Smooth over each motif to avoid wrinkling. Continue gluing and smoothing out wrinkles until the decoupage is complete. Allow the glue to dry completely.

6

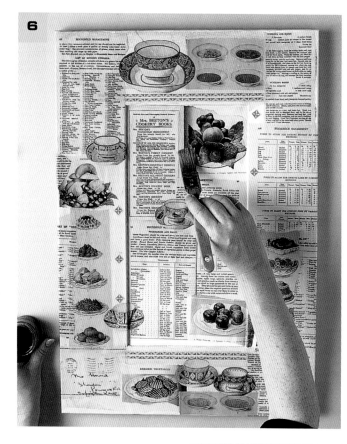

6 • APPLYING BUTTON POLISH SHELLAC

Use a varnish brush to apply a coat of button polish shellac, to seal the decoupage and add a honey-coloured, antiqued look to the door. Allow to dry thoroughly.

7

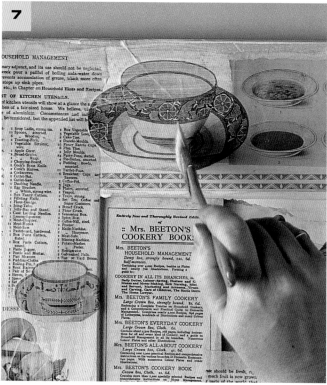

FURNITURE

A plain wooden knob, either new or antique, would be a suitably simple addition to this fun, eclectic design.

7 • FINISHING

Add two drops of white universal tinter to some matt acrylic varnish, and apply one coat with a varnish brush. When dry, apply two further coats of untinted matt varnish.

Neutral territory

The soft, delicate shades and subtle colour combinations of the natural and off-white palette are shown here in a range of different techniques and colour pairings. Cool coffee-and-cream crackle glaze, a colourwash in warm, sandstone hues, and rag-rolling in gentle creams are just a few of the designs that suit this colour palette particularly well.

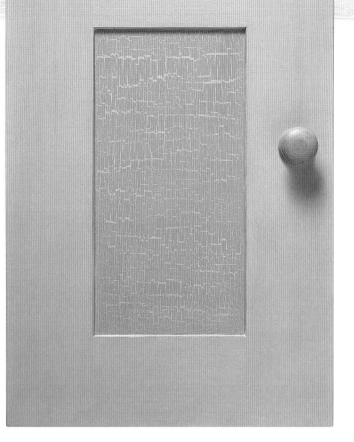

▲ COFFEE-AND-CREAM CRACKLE GLAZE

The subtle use of crackle glaze paired with soft coffee and cream colours creates a cool, contemporary style. After priming (see pages 6-9), paint the inner panel with two coats of mocha coffee matt emulsion or wood paint, and the outer panel with two coats of creamy coffee matt emulsion or wood paint. When dry, mask off the outer panel, then vertically brush crackle glaze onto the inner panel. Mix the two paints together to create a third, mid-tone colour, and paint horizontally over the dry crackle glaze, taking care not to brush over the same area twice. Once dry, seal with two coats of matt polyurethane varnish (see Polyurethane varnish, page 23).
Suitable for all surfaces.

◀ WILLOW-LEAF DECOUPAGE

This delicate design creates a restful, natural feel. After priming (see pages 6-9), apply two coats of ivory matt emulsion or wood paint. Use diluted PVA glue to stick the leaf skeletons firmly onto the door (see Step 5, page 39). Seal with white polish shellac, then apply three coats of matt acrylic varnish.
Suitable for wooden and MDF surfaces.

▼ CHECKED COLOURWASH

A sandstone colourwash applied in large checks creates this warm look. After priming (see pages 6-9), apply two coats of non-absorbent off-white matt emulsion or matt emulsion sealed with matt acrylic varnish. When dry, stick down horizontal rows of low-tack masking tape at 100mm (4 in) and 25mm (1 in) intervals. Mix a sandstone colourwash, then wash over the door (see Colourwashing, page 18). After 10 minutes, apply a stony-grey colourwash and drag through it following the thin tape lines (see Scumble glaze effects, page 19). When dry, stick down vertical rows of low-tack masking tape at the same intervals and repeat the colourwashing process. Remove the tape. After 24 hours, apply three coats of matt acrylic varnish.

Suitable for all surfaces.

▲ FROSTED-GLASS STENCIL

Glass doors get a new look with this simple faux etched and stencilled technique. Mask off the glass panel, prime the door frame (see pages 6-9) and apply two coats of milky chocolate matt emulsion. Remove the tape. Draw a selection of leaf motifs on stencil card, cut them out, then stick them onto the glass using low-tack adhesive spray, leaving spaces in between them. Mix a bit of white matt emulsion into some frosting medium and stipple around the leaves (see Step 6, page 49). When dry, carefully peel off the leaf motifs.

Suitable for clear glass-panelled doors with any type of frame.

▼ **SANDSTONE SPECKLE**

This technique recreates the grainy texture of stone. After priming (see pages 6-9), apply two coats of cream matt emulsion or wood paint. Mix four slightly different stone-coloured glazes to the consistency of milk, tinting them with varying amounts of raw umber, burnt sienna, and yellow ochre (see Scumble glaze effects, page 19). Mask off the outer panel and loosely paint the lightest glaze onto the inner panel. Stipple (see page 19), then spatter the remaining glazes (see Step 6, page 95). After 24 hours, apply three coats of matt acrylic varnish.

Suitable for all surfaces.

▲ **FILIGREE LEAF DESIGN**

A delicate filigree and distressed design. The door does not need priming. Rub candle wax onto parts of the door, then apply two coats of cream matt emulsion or wood paint. When dry, distress the mouldings and edges using coarse-grade sandpaper (see Distressing, page 18), then smooth with fine-grade sandpaper. Cut a piece of white card to fit the inner panel and coat the card with button polish shellac. Transfer a leaf design to the back of the card (see Step 6, page 36) and cut out using a scalpel. Discard the leaf shapes and leave the negative images. Apply a second coat of button polish shellac to the cutout. When dry, brush diluted PVA glue onto the inner panel. When tacky, smooth the cutout onto the panel, pressing firmly to avoid wrinkles. After one hour, seal with white polish shellac; apply a second coat after two hours. Leave overnight. Apply three coats of eggshell acrylic varnish.

Suitable for wooden surfaces.

▼ CREAM RAG-ROLL

A contemporary use of the rag-rolling technique. After priming (see pages 6-9), apply two coats of magnolia white matt emulsion. Mask off the dry outer panel. Paint the inner panel with pale yellow vinyl silk emulsion. Mix up a coffee cream glaze using ⅓ scumble glaze, ⅓ magnolia white emulsion and ⅓ eggshell acrylic varnish to the consistency of single cream, and tint with raw umber, yellow ochre and burnt sienna. Dip a rag into the glaze and roll over the panel (see Scumble glaze effects, page 19). When dry, remove the tape and apply three coats of matt acrylic varnish.

Suitable for all surfaces.

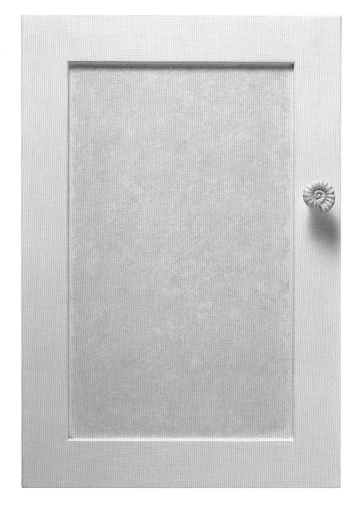

▲ PEN AND INK BARLEY STIPPLE

This barley motif brings a country feel to the kitchen. After priming (see pages 6-9), apply two coats of cream matt emulsion or wood paint. Mix equal proportions of colourwash and matt acrylic varnish (see Colourwashing, page 18) and tint to a warm sandstone using raw umber, burnt sienna and yellow ochre. Brush onto the door and stipple (see Scumble glaze effects, page 19); seal with matt acrylic varnish. Draw a barley design on tracing paper and transfer the design to the door (see Step 6, page 36). Go over the design with a black, fine, permanent, waterproof felt-tip pen. Dilute black wood paint with water and apply as a wash over parts of the motif to soften the design. Also add some sandstone as a thin wash. Create a border with two rows of low-tack masking tape and fill in with black paint. When dry, remove the tape and glide white polish shellac over the design. Apply three coats of eggshell acrylic varnish to the entire door.

Suitable for all surfaces.

YELLOWS & BROWNS

ONE OF THE MOST DIVERSE COLOURS IN THE DECORATOR'S PALETTE, YELLOW LENDS ITSELF TO A HOST OF TREATMENTS AND STYLES. ORANGEY-YELLOW SHADES BRING A SENSE OF LIVELINESS AND WARMTH TO A ROOM, ILLUMINATING

SMALL OR DREARY SPACES AND ENLIVENING BRIGHT, AIRY ONES. DUE TO THEIR HIGHER REFLECTIVE VALUE, PALER SHADES OF YELLOW OPEN UP SMALLER AREAS AND GIVE THEM A CHEERFUL LIFT. VIRTUALLY ALL SHADES WITHIN THE YELLOW PALETTE CAN BE MATCHED WITH A WIDE VARIETY OF OTHER COLOURS — WHITE, RED, BLUE, GREEN AND BLACK ARE SOME OF THE MOST POPULAR COMBINATIONS FOR THE KITCHEN. GOLD DETAILS OR ACCESSORIES AGAINST A YELLOW BACKGROUND ADD A HINT OF OPULENCE. TOWARDS THE DARKER END OF THE SPECTRUM, THE USE OF NATURAL EARTH COLOURS, WOODY TONES AND HONEY BROWNS IN A KITCHEN WILL IMBUE A SENSE OF WARMTH, COSINESS AND COMFORT.

Vine-leaf *stipple*

THIS EFFECT IS BASED ON the Victorian technique of 'fernwork', the fashion of stippling onto bare wood using an arrangement of leaves. When the leaf shapes are removed, a negative image is left, revealing the wood beneath.

We recreate the look here in a style that is both delicate and striking, using colours that result in an ambience ideal for kitchens lacking in warmth or character. Our design is based on the attractive vine-shaped leaves of *Parthenocissus*, or Virginia creeper, which lend themselves perfectly to this treatment. We have used a bare, sanded oak door, warmed up first with a honey-coloured polish, and finished with tawny and chestnut glazes. Different leaf shapes can be used; delicate and frond-like leaves tend to give the most pleasing effect.

MATERIALS AND EQUIPMENT

UNIVERSAL TINTERS: BURNT SIENNA, RAW UMBER, YELLOW OCHRE

RED ARTISTS' ACRYLIC PAINT

2 VARNISH BRUSHES

2 STENCIL BRUSHES

3 FINE ARTISTS' SABLE BRUSHES

SELECTION OF LEAVES

MAGAZINE OR NEWSPAPER

SEVERAL BOOKS OR OTHER HEAVY, FLAT OBJECTS

2 PAINT KETTLES

LOW-TACK SPRAY ADHESIVE

PAPER TOWEL

2 ELASTIC BANDS

SCALPEL

FINE-GRADE SANDPAPER

ACRYLIC SCUMBLE GLAZE

BUTTON POLISH SHELLAC

EGGSHELL ACRYLIC OR OIL-BASED VARNISH

1 • PREPARATION

This technique works best on bare, sanded, solid woods, such as oak or pine, but it can also be applied on painted wood, MDF, melamine, vinyl or laminate surfaces, although these will have less of a natural 'woody' appearance when finished. Prepare the surface following the instructions on pages 6-9. A few days prior to beginning, collect the leaves you intend to use and press them between the pages of a magazine or newspaper, weighted down under several books or other heavy, flat objects. Sand the door well, using fine-grade sandpaper.

2 • MIXING THE GLAZES

Just before you start, mix up a warm chestnut glaze and a lighter, tawny glaze as follows. Pour 20ml (4 tsp) of acrylic scumble glaze and 10ml (2 tsp) of water into two separate paint kettles. To make the chestnut glaze, add several drops of burnt sienna and raw umber; for the tawny glaze, add a few drops of yellow ochre and some burnt sienna and raw umber. Stir the glazes well, ensuring that the colourant is fully dispersed.

3

3 • SEALING THE WOOD

Using a varnish brush, carefully apply a coat of button polish shellac over the door's entire surface. Use long, even brushstrokes, letting the polish 'glide' over the surface. Take care not to overwork any one area — shellac is fast-drying, and quickly becomes tacky, so overbrushing will result in a rough, sticky surface. The polish seals the wood and adds a warm tone that suits this design. When fully dry, use fine-grade sandpaper to rub down any grain raised by the shellac. Brush or wipe away the sanding dust.

4 • CREATING THE DESIGN

Carefully remove the leaves, which should now be completely flat, from their makeshift press. Lay them out on the door in an arrangement you like. We used whole leaves of varying sizes for the central panel, and broke off single leaflets for the outer panel.

6 • STIPPLING ON THE GLAZES

Pour some of each glaze into separate saucers. Dip a dry stencil brush into the chestnut glaze, wiping off any excess on a paper towel. Wrap an elastic band around the base of the bristles for more control. Stipple – dabbing the brush onto the surface – the chestnut glaze around the leaves in the central panel, until the wood is covered. Do the same using the tawny glaze around the leaves on the outer panel.

5 • FIXING THE LEAVES

Remove a few leaves from a small section of the door. Spray them lightly with low-tack spray adhesive, and smooth each leaf back into position on the door. Move on to the next section, and continue carefully like this until all the leaves have been stuck down in position on the door.

7 • REMOVING THE LEAVES

As soon as all areas of the wood have been stippled, you can begin removing the leaves. Using a fingernail, or the pointed end of a scalpel, carefully pull up the tip of each leaf, then peel it back. If any leaves appear to be stuck, do not spend too long trying to remove them – peel off the remaining ones, then go back to the difficult ones and use a scalpel to lift or scrape them away.

7

TRADE SECRETS

- *Leaves that cannot be removed with a scalpel will loosen when dabbed with a cotton bud soaked in whatever solvent is recommended on the spray adhesive's label. Take care not to disturb the surrounding glaze.*

- *You may decide to hand-paint some detail, but resist the temptation to paint in the leaf veins. Doing so will make the design look fussy, and detract from the negative image you have created.*

8

8 • HAND-PAINTING

Any leaf shapes that appear blurred can now be touched up; use a fine artists' sable brush to paint in the missing detail with the appropriate glaze. Next, mix red artists' acrylic paint with some chestnut glaze, and paint in the rim between the central panel and the outer panel. Allow to dry fully.

9 • FINISHING

Apply another coat of button polish shellac, gliding it onto the door surface without overworking it. Once this has dried, you may need to sand the door lightly with fine-grade sandpaper for a completely smooth surface. Brush or vacuum away excess dust. Finish by varnishing with three coats of eggshell acrylic or oil-based varnish, allowing each coat to dry thoroughly before applying the next. If using oil-based varnish, sand lightly between coats.

FURNITURE

A shellacked wooden knob, perhaps decorated with a leaf motif, or a simple wrought-iron handle would work well with this design.

Textured *combing*

A MODERN INTERPRETATION of combing glazes, this effect will add a wonderfully rich texture to the surfaces of your cupboard doors, creating an overall look of contemporary chic. Simple to achieve, this technique involves applying a thick, paste-like paint onto a previously painted surface, and combing through it to reveal the colour beneath. This effect works especially well on doors that have an inner panel.

The use of different colour combinations will produce radically different effects; loud, bright colours will naturally create a very different look than softer, more muted tones. Here we use a combination of mochas, creams and browns, which blend together harmoniously to produce a soft corduroy look.

MATERIALS AND EQUIPMENT

MOCHA BROWN EMULSION
CREAM MATT EMULSION
COMBING PASTE OR CREAM EMULSION MIXED WITH
IMPASTO (OR SIMILARLY THICK TEXTURED PAINT),
AND ACRYLIC SCUMBLE GLAZE
UNIVERSAL TINTERS OR ARTISTS' ACRYLIC PAINTS:
BURNT UMBER, YELLOW OCHRE, WHITE
2 DECORATORS' PAINTBRUSHES
ARTISTS' SABLE BRUSH
VARNISH BRUSH
LOW-TACK MASKING TAPE
10MM (⅜ IN) LOW-TACK LINING TAPE
PAINT KETTLE
RUBBER DECORATING COMB
FINE-GRADE SANDPAPER
MATT ACRYLIC VARNISH
EGGSHELL ACRYLIC VARNISH (OPTIONAL)

1 • PREPARATION

This technique is only suitable for solid wood and MDF doors – it is not appropriate for melamine, vinyl or laminate doors. Prepare the surface following the instructions on pages 6-9. Apply two coats of mocha brown emulsion, allowing plenty of time for drying in between, and sanding between coats using fine-grade sandpaper. When dry, use a varnish brush to apply a coat of matt acrylic varnish. Allow to dry, then mask off the moulding and outer panel with low-tack masking tape.

2 • MIXING THE PASTE

If you are using a ready-made combing paste, tint it with white, burnt umber and yellow ochre universal tinters or artists' acrylic paints to produce a soft cream colour. If a ready-made paste is unavailable, you can create a similar mixture using one part cream matt emulsion, one part impasto (or similarly thick textured paint) and one part acrylic scumble glaze. Tint this mixture as described above. Make sure that either mixture is adequately stirred.

3

3 • APPLYING THE PASTE

Using a household paintbrush, apply a thick, even layer of combing paste to the door's inner panel using smooth vertical brushstrokes. Make sure that the paste is distributed evenly over the panel. Work on one door at a time.

4 • COMBING

Begin combing immediately after the paste has been applied. Starting at the left side of the panel, grip the comb with both hands and drag it down through the paste. Exert a firm, even pressure, keeping the movement as straight as possible. As you comb down through each section, overlap the comb's teeth by one notch, and repeat the same dragging action, until the entire inner panel has been combed. Leave to dry for at least 24 hours at room temperature, then carefully peel back the masking tape.

4

5

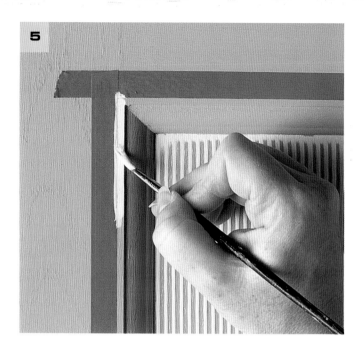

5 • FRAMING THE INNER PANEL

Frame the textured inner panel by hand-painting a cream line at the edge of the door's moulding. Stick two lines of 10mm (⅜ in) low-tack lining tape to the edge of the moulding, about 6mm (¼ in) apart. Using an artists' sable brush, apply two coats of cream matt emulsion between the tape lines, allowing the first coat to dry before painting the second. When the paint has dried, carefully remove the tape.

6 • FINISHING

Using a varnish brush, apply three coats of matt acrylic varnish, allowing each coat to dry thoroughly before applying the next. Or, if you wish to soften the textured look further, use an eggshell acrylic varnish to achieve a flatter, more unified effect.

6

FURNITURE

Complement this finish with a simple bronze or brass handle or knob – the contrasting smoothness will highlight the rich texture.

Birch woodgraining
with *faux ebony & ivory inlay*

Faux woodgraining is an established way of transforming inexpensive and unexciting pieces of furniture and plywood panels into stylish, expensive-looking items. Imitations of pale woodgrains such as maple and birch are particularly fashionable for contemporary kitchen spaces, creating an ambience that is crisp and bright, as well as elegant and stylish.

Inexpensive and simple to achieve, this technique offers a fabulous solution to converting dull and lifeless kitchen cupboards into modern, exciting ones. To complete this look, embellish the grained surface with a thin black and white line painted to look like an ebony and ivory inlay.

MATERIALS AND EQUIPMENT

IVORY MATT EMULSION OR HIGHLY PIGMENTED
WOOD PAINT

UNIVERSAL TINTERS: YELLOW OCHRE, RAW UMBER,
BURNT SIENNA, WHITE

ARTISTS' ACRYLIC PAINTS: WHITE, BLACK

2 DECORATORS' PAINTBRUSHES

VARNISH BRUSH

FLOGGING BRUSH

PENCIL OVERGRAINER

BADGER-HAIR SOFTENER

3 FINE ARTISTS' SABLE BRUSHES

13MM (½ IN) ONE-STROKE BRUSH, SABLE OR NYLON

RULER

PENCIL

13MM (½ IN) LOW-TACK LINING OR MASKING TAPE

PAINT KETTLE

FINE-GRADE SANDPAPER

ACRYLIC SCUMBLE GLAZE

EGGSHELL ACRYLIC VARNISH

MATT ACRYLIC VARNISH

1 • PREPARATION

This treatment can be used on MDF, melamine, vinyl, laminate and close-grained wooden doors (an open grain should be filled and sanded – see page 9).

Prepare the surface following the instructions on pages 6-9. Apply two coats of ivory matt emulsion or wood paint, leaving the first coat to dry completely before applying the second. Sand lightly between coats using fine-grade sandpaper on wooden and MDF doors. Paint as evenly as possible – it is important to obtain a flat, smooth surface. When completely dry, use a varnish brush to apply a coat of eggshell acrylic varnish. Allow to dry thoroughly.

2 • APPLYING THE FIRST GLAZE

Mix up a pale creamy glaze as follows: spoon two parts acrylic scumble glaze into a paint kettle and make up the final third with equal parts of water and matt acrylic varnish. Tint with two to three drops of yellow ochre, one drop of raw umber, one drop of burnt sienna and two drops of white universal tinter. Paint on the glaze using loose brushstrokes.

3

3 • FLOGGING AND OVERGRAINING

Take the flogging brush and, working upwards from the bottom of the door, flog over the still-wet glaze – hitting the brush flatly onto the surface – until a consistent, flecked effect has been achieved. Pull the pencil overgrainer down through the damp glaze in wavy lines, repeatedly wiping the excess glaze from the brush. Soften with a badger-hair softener, brushing lightly in all directions. Allow to dry thoroughly.

TRADE SECRETS

- *When painting woodgrain finishes, obtain a sample or photograph of the wood you are recreating to use as a reference, and practise the technique on cardboard before working directly on the actual surface.*

- *Keep all grain lines and mottling patterns as simple and subtle as possible: remember that 'less is more'.*

4

4 • PAINTING IN THE GRAIN

Mix up a mid-tone brown glaze using the same proportions of glaze, water and matt acrylic varnish as in the first glaze, and, using universal tinters, tint with one drop of burnt sienna, one drop of yellow ochre and half a drop of raw umber. Using a fine artists' sable brush, paint in the lighter lines of the grain with this glaze. Loosely follow the lines created by the pencil overgrainer, softening frequently with the badger-hair softener. The lines should be long and tapering, travelling the width or length of each panel, with occasional 'heartgrain' shapes. Refer to real birch for inspiration.

FURNITURE

A slender brass handle or a plain black knob would best suit this effect.

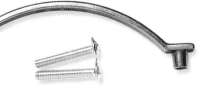

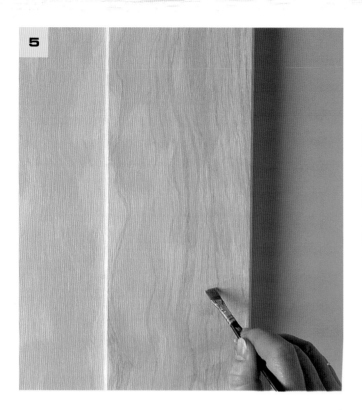

5 • MOTTLING

Dilute the mid-tone brown glaze used for the grain lines with water to make a transparent wash. Use a 13mm (½ in) one-stroke brush to apply a small amount of this wash in short, soft marks, at a horizontal angle to a few of the grain lines — like a subtle zebra print. Soften these marks with the softener as you work. Add a tapering shadow to the 'heartgrain' shapes; this will make the grain lines appear less distinct, lending extra depth. Allow to dry for at least 24 hours. Apply a coat of eggshell acrylic varnish to seal and protect, and allow to dry for another 24 hours.

6 • CREATING THE FAUX INLAY

Draw a fine pencil guideline through the middle of the outer panel of the door, all the way around the door. Use a ruler to ensure straight lines. Stick a strip of 13mm (½ in) low-tack lining or masking tape on both sides of the guideline, leaving a 6mm (¼ in) gap. Using an artists' sable brush, paint in the line with white artists' acrylic paint. Allow to dry thoroughly.

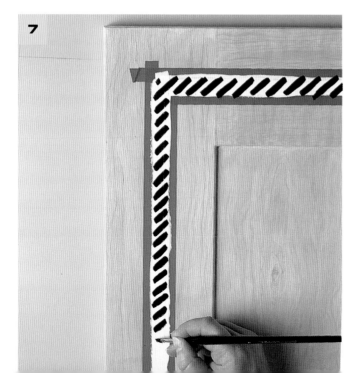

7 • COMPLETING THE FAUX INLAY

Add small black diagonal flecks to the white line using black artists' acrylic paint, creating equal diagonal lines of black and white. Carefully peel off the tape, and leave until completely dry.

8 • FINISHING

Apply three coats of eggshell acrylic varnish to seal and protect, allowing each coat to dry thoroughly before applying the next. Brush the varnish out as evenly as possible, so that brush marks are not visible on the finished effect.

Gold *craquelure*

GOLD ALWAYS EXUDES WARMTH when used in interiors, but it can sometimes be a little overbearing and grand for its surroundings. To lighten the look, gold can be used as an embellishment to a lighter colour scheme, combining modern materials and traditional styles, as we have done here. The result is a charming kitchen design possessing both the richness of gold and a subtlety of colour. When applied to an entire kitchen, this colour scheme creates a warm, elegant ambience while still retaining a sense of comfort and spaciousness.

MATERIALS AND EQUIPMENT

IVORY MATT EMULSION OR HIGHLY PIGMENTED
WOOD PAINT

SAND SUEDE-EFFECT PAINT OR MATT
HIGHLY PIGMENTED WOOD PAINT

GOLD ARTISTS' OIL PAINT

YELLOW OCHRE UNIVERSAL TINTER

2 DECORATORS' PAINTBRUSHES

5 VARNISH BRUSHES

LOW-TACK MASKING TAPE

LINT-FREE CLOTH

WHITE SPIRIT

PAINT KETTLE

FINE-GRADE SANDPAPER

WHITE POLISH SHELLAC

TWO-PART CRAQUELURE VARNISH

ACRYLIC EGGSHELL VARNISH

METALLIC ACRYLIC VARNISH

1 • PREPARATION

This technique is only suitable for solid wood and MDF doors – it is unsuitable for melamine, vinyl or laminate surfaces. Prepare the surface following the instructions on pages 6-9. Apply two coats of ivory matt emulsion or wood paint to the inner panel, letting the first coat dry before applying the second, and sanding between coats using fine-grade sandpaper. Allow to dry thoroughly.

2 • PAINTING THE BORDER

Use low-tack masking tape to mask off the inner panel. Paint the outer panel with sand suede-effect paint; if this type of paint is not available, use a very matt wood paint. Leave until completely dry.

3 • APPLYING THE VARNISH

Remove the masking tape from the inner panel and mask off the outer panel. Using a varnish brush, apply the first step of the craquelure varnish. Brush it on evenly, making sure no corners or edges have been missed. Allow to dry completely.

Paint on the second step of the varnish with a clean varnish brush, brushing on a medium-thick, even coat. Leave overnight to dry completely.

4 • HIGHLIGHTING THE CRACKS

Squeeze some gold artists' oil paint onto a lint-free cloth and rub it over the dry craquelure, making sure it gets into all the cracks. Rub back the oil paint with a clean cloth so that the colour remains in the cracks only. You will need to switch to a new clean cloth several times. If the oil paint remains steadfast, pour a small amount of white spirit onto a clean cloth and rub it lightly over the surface, leaving the gold in the cracks intact. Rub down again with a clean cloth. Allow to dry for 24 hours.

5 • SEALING AND VARNISHING

Using a clean varnish brush, seal the craquelure panel with a coat of white polish shellac. Once this has dried, apply three coats of acrylic eggshell varnish, allowing each coat to dry thoroughly before applying the next.

TRADE SECRETS

- *Do not confuse crackle glaze and craquelure varnishes. Craquelure is a two-step varnish that produces hairline cracks in the varnish coat, while crackle glaze is sandwiched between two layers of paint, and causes the top coat of paint to crack.*

- *The size of the cracks made by craquelure varnish will be determined by the thickness of the second coat. Brush the varnish on thickly to achieve larger cracks, or apply a thinner coat for smaller cracks.*

6 • APPLYING TINTED METALLIC VARNISH

Pour some metallic acrylic varnish into a paint kettle and tint with two drops of yellow ochre universal tinter. Stir thoroughly. Mask off the inner panel, and, using a clean varnish brush, paint the tinted metallic varnish onto the outer panel using smooth, even strokes. This final touch will give the door frame a beautiful gold, pearlescent lustre.

FURNITURE

Antiqued brass or gold knobs and fittings mirror the richness, opulence and warmth of the gold hue.

Sunny side up

Here we see the remarkable versatility of the yellow and brown palette. Some beautiful techniques in this colour range are shown here, including a sunny yellow plaster finish, decoupage and craquelure in warm orange tones and luxurious gold effects.

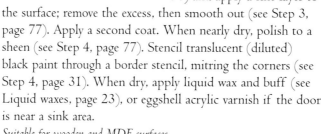

▲ LINEN STENCIL AND EMBROIDERY SAMPLER

The golden amber tones of this effect create a warming ambience. After priming (see pages 6-9), apply two coats of pale yellow matt emulsion or wood paint to the outer panel and warm orange to the inner panel. When dry, stencil warm orange through a fine mesh linen stencil on the outer panel, working in circular strokes. Seal a colour photocopy of a yellow or an orange embroidery sampler with white polish shellac; when dry, cut to fit the door panel. Stick the photocopy smoothly onto the panel with diluted PVA glue (see Step 5, page 39). When dry, apply button polish shellac to the whole door. After 24 hours, apply eggshell polyurethane varnish (see Polyurethane varnish, page 23).

Suitable for all surfaces.

◀ POLISHED PLASTER AND STENCIL

The lustre of polished plaster tinted to a warm yellow is highlighted with a sophisticated black border stencil. After priming (see pages 6-9), apply two coats of yellow matt emulsion. Tint some polished plaster with yellow (see Step 2, page 76) and apply a fine layer to the surface; remove the excess, then smooth out (see Step 3, page 77). Apply a second coat. When nearly dry, polish to a sheen (see Step 4, page 77). Stencil translucent (diluted) black paint through a border stencil, mitring the corners (see Step 4, page 31). When dry, apply liquid wax and buff (see Liquid waxes, page 23), or eggshell acrylic varnish if the door is near a sink area.

Suitable for wooden and MDF surfaces.

▼ DECOUPAGE AND CRAQUELURE

A warm, rustic, country-style design. After priming (see pages 6-9), apply two coats of cream matt non-absorbent emulsion or emulsion sealed with matt acrylic varnish, then wash over with a terracotta colourwash (see Colourwashing, page 18). After 24 hours, seal with matt acrylic varnish. Seal fruit decoupage motifs with white polish shellac and cut out (see Step 5, page 39). Stick the motifs onto the inner panel with diluted PVA glue (see Step 2, page 38). Seal with button polish shellac. When dry, mask off the outer panel and apply both steps of the craquelure varnish to the inner panel. When dry, rub raw umber artists' oil paint into the cracks (see Steps 3 and 4, page 61). After 24 hours, seal with white polish shellac. Remove the tape. Apply three coats of matt acrylic varnish.

Suitable for all surfaces.

▲ YELLOW COLOURWASH AND SUNFLOWER STAMP

Cheery sunflowers on a yellow colourwashed background create a lively, radiant look. After priming (see pages 6-9), apply two coats of warm yellow non-absorbent emulsion or emulsion sealed with matt acrylic varnish, then wash with a bright yellow ochre-coloured colourwash (see Colourwashing, page 18). After 24 hours, seal with acrylic matt varnish. Use artists' acrylic paints to stamp sunflower and leaf motifs onto the door (see Steps 6–8, pages 73–74). Hand-paint highlights on the petals and seeds using bright yellow and burnt sienna artists' acrylic paints; use green to hand-paint the leaves. For the stems, tape lines of low-tack lining tape and paint in. When dry, apply three coats of matt acrylic varnish.

Suitable for all surfaces.

▼ MARQUETRY STYLE

Warm tones and a classic inlay design are paired together for a country feel. There is no need to prime the door. Sand the door, then draw out the design in pencil. Use a metal ruler and scalpel to score the design into the wood (see Step 3, page 81). Paint in the design using light oak, dark oak and red mahogany oil-based wood stains. Allow to dry overnight. Seal with two coats of button polish shellac; allow to dry between coats. After 24 hours, apply three coats of eggshell acrylic varnish.

Suitable for bare or stripped wooden surfaces such as pine or oak.

▲ VINEGAR GLAZE AND CLING FILM FROTTAGE

The woody tones of this glaze are combined here with a contemporary gloss finish for a bold, rich style. After priming (see pages 6-9), apply two coats of straw-coloured emulsion or wood paint and seal with white polish shellac. Mix a vinegar glaze to the consistency of milk using burnt sienna and raw umber pigments (see Step 2, page 112). Mask off the outer panel and apply the glaze to the inner panel (see Step 3, page 113). Tear a length of cling film and lay it over the wet glaze, scrunching it up slightly. Pat it down all over, then pull it back. Remove the tape and repeat, using new cling film, on the outer panel. When dry, carefully glide on white polish shellac. After 24 hours, apply three coats of gloss acrylic varnish.

Suitable for wooden and MDF surfaces.

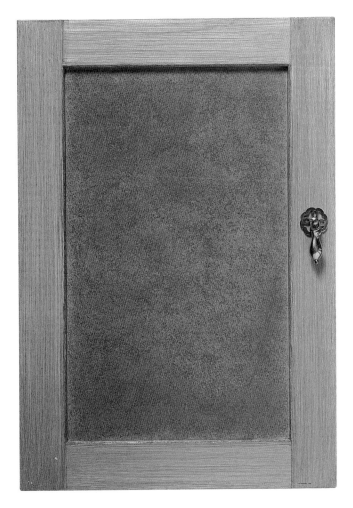

▼ HAND-PAINTED STRIPES

Simple hand-painted stripes produce instant style. After priming (see pages 6-9), apply two coats of pale yellow matt emulsion or wood paint. Stick down two rows of low-tack masking tape around the door's edge. Paint freehand stripes using three different shades of yellow paint (see Choosing colours, page 24, for guidance); use three different brushes for varying widths. Don't worry if the stripes wobble – it's all part of the effect. When dry, remove the tape and apply three coats of matt acrylic varnish.

Suitable for all surfaces.

▲ TAWNY STIPPLING AND SPONGING

Earthy amber tones create a simple, warming effect. After priming (see pages 6-9), apply two coats of ivory-cream matt emulsion or wood paint. Mix two acrylic glazes to the consistency of single cream: mix a lighter one using yellow ochre, burnt sienna and raw umber, and use the same colours, but add more burnt sienna, for a darker one. Mask off the outer panel. Apply the lighter glaze to the inner panel. Stipple (see Scumble glaze effects, page 19) and leave to dry. Dip a damp sea sponge into the darker glaze and dab over the stippled panel, leaving some of the lighter glaze showing through. Soften with a badger-hair softener. Remove the tape from the outer panel and, when dry, mask off the inner panel. Drag the lighter glaze through the outer panel (see Acrylic glaze effects, page 19). When dry, apply three coats of matt acrylic varnish.

Suitable for wooden and MDF surfaces.

▼ **CRAQUELURE ON COPPER LEAF**

Combine copper leaf with craquelure for fiery undertones. After priming (see pages 6-9), apply a coat of deep yellow matt emulsion or wood paint. Mask off the outer panel and apply white polish shellac to the inner panel. Gild copper transfer metal leaf to cover the inner panel; seal with white polish shellac (see Steps 4-7, page 117). When dry, apply both steps of craquelure varnish. After a few hours, rub burnt sienna artists' oil paint into the cracks (see Step 4, page 61). Remove the tape and rub burnt sienna artists' oil paint onto the outer panel. Leave overnight, then seal with button polish shellac. When dry, apply three coats of semi-gloss acrylic varnish to the whole door and rub light brown shoe polish onto the outer panel.

Suitable for wooden and MDF surfaces.

▲ **GOLD CHECKS**

After priming (see pages 6-9), apply two coats of cream matt emulsion or wood paint. Mark a grid of four squares across the width of the inner panel in pencil; seal with white polish shellac. Cut out gold transfer metal leaf squares and gild alternate squares (see Steps 4-6, page 117). Apply three coats of button polish shellac to the gilding. Tint metallic varnish yellow; apply three coats to the ungilded squares and door frame.

Suitable for wooden and MDF surfaces.

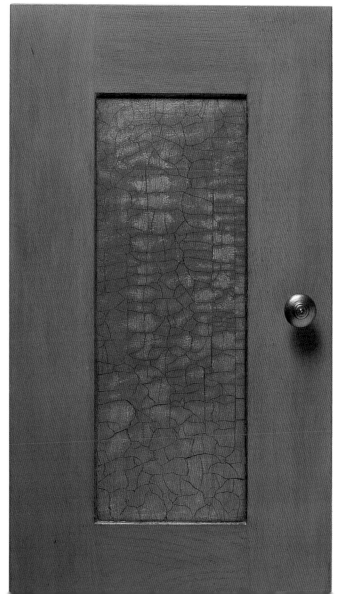

▼ HAND-PAINTED GOLD PANEL

An exquisite hand-painted door in the style of a traditional Japanese screen. After priming (see pages 6-9), apply two coats of light terracotta matt emulsion or wood paint. Mask off the outer panel and apply white polish shellac to the inner panel. Gild gold transfer metal leaf to cover the whole panel and seal with white polish shellac (see Steps 4-7, page 117). Mix a brown and a red paint using artists' acrylic paints and hand-paint brown branches and red blossom. Remove the tape and rub red wax onto the frame and gilding wax onto the moulding, then buff (see Coloured wax and Gilding wax, page 23). Varnish the inner panel with two coats of satin polyurethane varnish (see Polyurethane varnish, page 23). *Suitable for wooden and MDF surfaces.*

▲ GOLD RELIEF STENCILLING

The mellow tones of antiqued gold and apricot create a feeling of luxury and warmth. Apply one coat of pale yellow non-absorbent matt emulsion or matt emulsion sealed with matt acrylic varnish and rub back with medium-grade sandpaper to reveal some of the wood. Stencil a linear border with impasto or a thick-textured paint (see Step 3, page 31). When dry, sand any rough edges (see Step 5, page 31). Mix an apricot colourwash and wash over the whole door (see Colourwashing, page 18). When dry, seal the raised stencilling with white polish shellac. Gild gold transfer metal leaf onto the raised areas and seal with white polish shellac (see Steps 4-7, page 117). When dry, apply three coats of eggshell acrylic varnish to the whole door. Rub in dark brown shoe polish and buff. *Suitable for wooden surfaces.*

REDS

No matter what the shade, the colour red always has a dramatic and immediate impact on a room. It is also one of the best colours for creating a warm, welcoming ambience. Bright reds, berry hues and terracotta shades lend a lived-in, cosy atmosphere. A versatile colour, red is striking, yet subtle when used for broken-colour finishes such as distressing, colorwashing and polished plaster effects; it can also be used as a bold note within patterns. Black and cream are both attractive accent colours against a red background. Muted, pastel green shades placed near red will soften the boldness of its impact. The addition of copper and gold metallic effects can be used to enhance the appearance of a warm shade of red; copper will bring out the colour's fiery undertones, while gold will create a luxurious, opulent highlight.

Mulberry colourwash
& repeat stamping

COLOURWASHING is a popular and widely used technique for creating a beautiful, soft bloom of broken colour with far greater depth than plain, flat-painting. Equally effective on furniture and walls, it is a simple finish with classic appeal that lends itself to both modern and traditional settings. Above all, it is a relatively quick and easy way to give kitchen doors a facelift at very little cost.

Here we introduce deep, rich berry tones, with a repeat stamp motif in gold and a brown shadow. The soft beauty of this design in these colours will add a warm and welcoming glow to kitchens large and small.

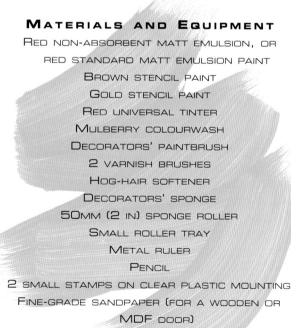

MATERIALS AND EQUIPMENT

RED NON-ABSORBENT MATT EMULSION, OR
RED STANDARD MATT EMULSION PAINT
BROWN STENCIL PAINT
GOLD STENCIL PAINT
RED UNIVERSAL TINTER
MULBERRY COLOURWASH
DECORATORS' PAINTBRUSH
2 VARNISH BRUSHES
HOG-HAIR SOFTENER
DECORATORS' SPONGE
50MM (2 IN) SPONGE ROLLER
SMALL ROLLER TRAY
METAL RULER
PENCIL
2 SMALL STAMPS ON CLEAR PLASTIC MOUNTING
FINE-GRADE SANDPAPER (FOR A WOODEN OR MDF DOOR)
MATT ACRYLIC VARNISH

1 • PREPARATION

Colourwash is ideally suited to solid wood and MDF doors, but will also work on melamine, vinyl or laminate surfaces. Prepare the surface following the instructions on pages 6-9. Use an acrylic or melamine primer, or an acrylic convertor (according to door type) and tint with eight to ten drops of red universal tinter, to produce a red-toned primer. Apply a thin, even coat to the door, and allow to dry fully. Apply a second coat. Again, allow to dry fully. Sand between coats on wooden and MDF doors using fine-grade sandpaper.

2 • PAINTING THE BASE COAT

Apply two even coats of red matt emulsion to the door, allowing plenty of time for drying in between. Use a non-absorbent matt emulsion, or, if unavailable, seal a standard matt emulsion with a coat of matt acrylic varnish to make the surface non-absorbent. Sand between coats using fine-grade sandpaper on wooden and MDF doors. Allow a full 24 hours for the paint to cure before applying the colourwash.

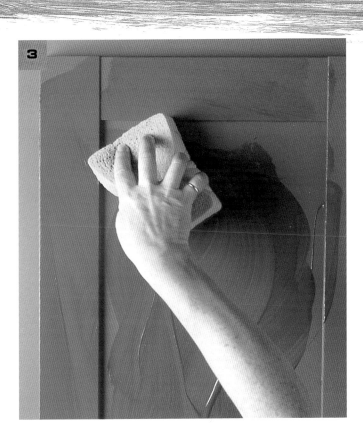

3 • APPLYING THE COLOURWASH

Working on one door at a time, pour approximately 15ml (1 tbsp) of mulberry colourwash onto a decorators' sponge. Use the sponge to wipe the colourwash onto the door in swirling figure-of-eight movements, until completely covered. Make sure that there are no gaps in the colourwash.

4 • SOFTENING THE COLOURWASH

Immediately take the hog-hair softener and brush softly over the colourwash in light, sweeping criss-cross movements, softening and blending the wash. The glaze will quickly become sticky, so you need to work swiftly at this stage. Allow to dry for at least 12 hours.

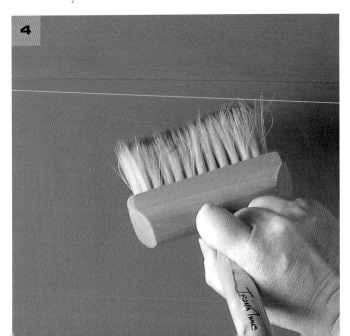

5 • VARNISHING

Apply a coat of matt acrylic varnish with a varnish brush, gliding it onto the surface. This seals the colourwash and makes the surface wipeable, a life-saver if you make a mistake during the stamping process. Allow to dry thoroughly. To add extra depth to the colour, apply another colourwash following the instructions in Steps 3-4; varnish again to seal.

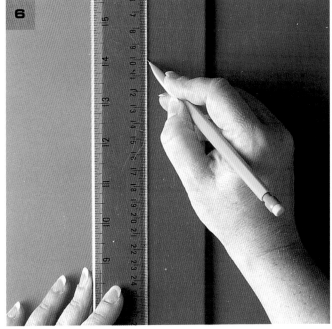

6 • MARKING UP FOR STAMPING

Small repeat motifs are an effective way to introduce a pattern that won't dominate the overall effect. Measure the outer panel of the door and mark the position of the stamping repeats with small pencil dots at regular intervals. Measure and mark the inner panel so that the stamp is repeated between two and three times on each line, creating a diamond repeat pattern. For our design, we used the flower part of the stamp for the outer panel, and both the flower and stem sections of the stamp together for the inner panel.

7 • INKING UP THE STAMP

Pour some brown stencil paint into a small roller tray. Work a 50mm (2 in) sponge roller forwards and backwards through the paint until it is evenly distributed on the roller. Roll the paint evenly onto the stamp. Do not overload the stamp, as this will cause the paint to bleed and smudge when you press it onto the surface.

8 • FIRST STAMPING – THE SHADOW

Press the stamp onto the surface, positioning it centrally on one of the pencil dots. Continue inking the stamp and printing in the same way, until you have covered all of the pencil marks. Stamp the inner panel first, starting at the top left-hand corner if you are right-handed, or at the top right-hand corner if you are left-handed, to avoid smudging. Then stamp the pattern onto the outer panel. Allow to dry thoroughly.

9 • SECOND STAMPING – THE HIGHLIGHT

Clean and dry the roller and stamp. Ink up the stamp with gold stencil paint. To highlight the shadow below, place the stamp slightly to the right of the brown stamped motif already created – the clear plastic mounting of the stamp will make a good registration guide. Repeat over all of the previous stamping, and leave the paint to dry thoroughly.

10 • FINISHING

Varnish the door with two coats of matt acrylic varnish, allowing the first coat to dry thoroughly before applying the second.

FURNITURE

Burnished or antiqued brass or gold-effect knobs or handles will reflect the highlights and warm, rich hues of this design.

TRADE SECRETS

- *When painting a melamine or vinyl surface, be sure to leave adequate drying time between coats. Doing so will enhance the bonding process, making the finish more durable.*

- *The stamp must be pressed firmly down perpendicular to the surface, or the edges of the image may turn out fuzzy. The best way to ensure a straight image is to stand directly behind the stamp, not to the side of it – this will help you line it up with maximum accuracy.*

Terracotta polished plaster
& copper squares

POLISHED PLASTER CREATES a classical finish for both traditional and contemporary interiors, adding a lustrous depth and sheen that is hard to achieve with paint alone. Also known as marmorino, stucco, Venetian plaster, Swedish putty or brushing putty, polished plaster contains marble dust, making it possible to create the look of real, polished marble; the resulting effect is sumptuous, highly distinctive elegance. Although it takes a bit of practice and time to apply, the results of this finish are truly rewarding.

Here we work with polished plaster that has been tinted to a rich terracotta colour. The plaster is then given extra sheen with a ruby-coloured wax, and copper highlights are added for a contemporary twist.

1 • PREPARATION
This technique is only suitable for solid wood or MDF doors – it is unsuitable for melamine, vinyl or laminate surfaces. Sand the door using fine-grade sandpaper, then seal it with slightly diluted PVA glue. Apply an even coat of acrylic primer. When dry, sand down any ridges.

2 • TINTING THE PLASTER
You will need about 90ml (6 tbsp) of polished plaster for an average-sized cupboard door. Put the plaster into a plastic paint kettle, add four to five drops each of red and burnt sienna universal tinters and stir thoroughly, until all of the colour has been mixed in.

MATERIALS AND EQUIPMENT
ACRYLIC PRIMER
POLISHED PLASTER
UNIVERSAL TINTERS: RED, BURNT SIENNA
FITCH BRUSH
DECORATORS' PAINTBRUSH
ARTISTS' SABLE BRUSH
DECORATORS' STEEL FLOAT
COPPER TRANSFER METAL LEAF
ACRYLIC GILDING SIZE
PAINT KETTLE
RULER
PENCIL
SHARP SCISSORS
CARDBOARD
LINT-FREE CLOTH
PVA GLUE
FINE-GRADE SANDPAPER
CLEAR BEESWAX POLISH
RED-TINTED WAX POLISH
WHITE POLISH SHELLAC

TRADE SECRETS

- *Plaster may crack if applied too thickly. Practise the technique on a piece of board before applying it to a door.*

- *A wax finish is not suitable around sinks or areas that may get wet. As an alternative, apply one coat of gloss acrylic varnish tinted with one to two drops of red universal tinter. Brush on evenly, working around the copper squares. Apply a second coat of clear, untinted gloss varnish over the entire surface of the door, including the copper squares.*

3 • APPLYING THE FIRST LAYER

Spoon 45ml (3 tbsp) of the plaster onto the top edge of a decorators' steel float, and smooth it onto the entire surface of the door in wide, arcing movements. Make sure that the entire surface is covered evenly with the plaster, which should be about 3mm (⅛ in) thick, and that no plaster is wrapped around the sides. After making the surface as smooth as possible, leave for 10-15 minutes, then return and smooth again with the edge of the float, removing any excess plaster or ridges. Allow to dry a little more, then smooth over once again.

4 • APPLYING THE SECOND LAYER

When the first layer of plaster is almost dry (it will be cold to the touch), apply a second coat, about 3mm (⅛ in) thick, as before. Leave for about 10 minutes, then return and smooth over. Return thereafter at 5-10 minute intervals and smooth, applying a firmer pressure to the float each time. With each successive smoothing process, a natural sheen will begin to appear. The more effort put in at this stage, the higher the lustre. Allow to dry completely for 24 hours.

5 • MARKING UP

Use a ruler and a pencil to mark up 25mm (1 in) squares on the back of the copper transfer sheets, then cut out with a pair of sharp scissors. You will need about ten squares per door. Cut out a 100mm (4 in) cardboard square to use as a template. Turn the cardboard onto the diagonal, and position it so that it can fit into the width of your door roughly twice (if it fits in more than twice, increase the size of your template accordingly). Starting about 40mm (1½ in) from the top of the door, draw pencil dots at the corners of the cardboard. Mark up the entire door in this way. Draw a 25mm (1 in) square around each dot, centring it.

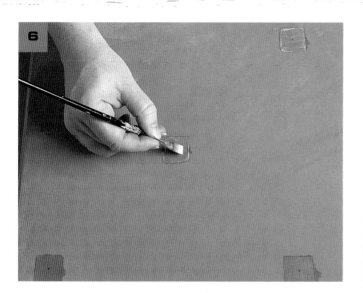

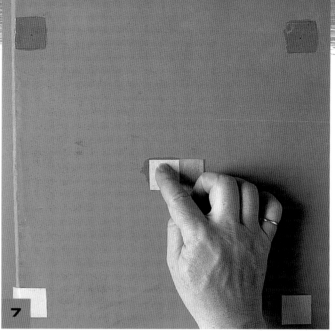

6 • APPLYING GILDING SIZE

Using a fitch brush, apply a small amount of white polish shellac to each square to seal that area of the plaster. Allow to dry thoroughly, then use an artists' sable brush to add a fine, even layer of acrylic gilding size to each square. Leave for about 15 minutes, or until the size becomes translucent.

FURNITURE

A terracotta knob with a copper square detail is the ideal match for this design. If drilling the knob in, stick masking tape to the door's surface and carefully drill through to prevent the plaster from cracking.

7 • APPLYING THE COPPER LEAF

Carefully press the copper leaf squares onto the sized squares, rubbing the transfer backing paper carefully with your finger to ensure the copper adheres fully. Carefully peel away the transfer backing paper. Seal each square with a small amount of white polish shellac, and leave to dry.

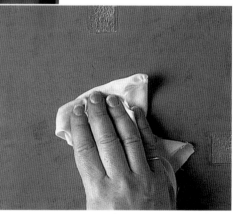

8 • FINISHING

Using a lint-free cloth, apply clear beeswax polish to the door, carefully working around the copper squares. The polish will be readily absorbed into the porous surface of the plaster. Gently remove the excess wax, then buff. Apply a thin coat of red-tinted wax polish, again avoiding the copper squares. Remove any excess wax, then buff up to a full sheen. The effort put into polishing at this stage will be significant — the more you buff, the deeper the sheen.

Limed finish
on *marquetry-style wood paint*

Liming adds a beautiful silvery bloom to open-grained hardwoods such as oak and ash, and softens and lightens the look of woods that otherwise may appear heavy or drab. The limed look has a timeless appeal, and brings classic distinction to any kitchen.

Here we use a modern liming paste – which doesn't have the caustic properties of traditional slaked lime. Because liming paste can be varnished, it is especially appropriate for the kitchen. A coloured marquetry-style design has been added before liming the doors for an exceptionally stylish and unique overall look.

1 • PREPARATION
This technique is only suitable for hardwood doors with an open grain – it is unsuitable for melamine, vinyl or laminate surfaces, and for soft woods, such as pine. Older wood must be stripped and sanded down (see pages 8-9). Do not prime the doors.

2 • OPENING UP THE GRAIN
Use a stiff wire brush to 'rake' out the grain, brushing firmly and always working in the direction of the grain. Brush off, then wipe with a damp cloth to remove all loose matter.

MATERIALS AND EQUIPMENT
Highly pigmented wood paint or acrylic wood stains: red, orange, yellow
Stiff wire brush
Decorator's paintbrush
2 varnish brushes
13mm (½ in) one-stroke brush, sable or nylon
Artists' sable brush
Dusting brush
Small soft wire brush – as used on suede
Liming paste
2 damp cloths
Metal ruler
Pencil
Sharp scalpel
Dust mask
Fine-grade sandpaper
White polish shellac
Matt acrylic varnish

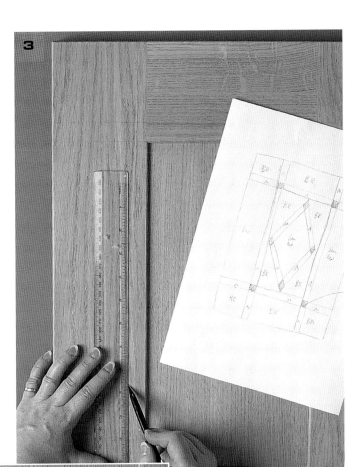

4 • PAINTING THE DESIGN

Dilute three wood paint colours, using three parts water to two parts wood paint, or use acrylic wood stain colours. We used a rich berry red, guava orange and warm yellow. Paint the wood paint or stain onto the door as evenly as possible, brushing in the direction of the grain. Use a 13mm (½ in) one-stroke brush for large areas, and an artists' sable brush for fine lines and edges. Allow to dry fully.

5 • APPLYING THE LIMING PASTE

Stir the liming paste well before use. With a decorators' paintbrush, apply a thick, even coat of paste over the door, painting in the direction of the grain. The paste will mask the design beneath, but don't worry, it will be revealed again later. Leave the paste to dry for one hour, or until completely dry.

3 • DRAWING AND SCORING THE DESIGN

Choose a simple geometric design for your door based on diamonds or squares. Make a rough plan of the design first, then transfer it to the door using a ruler and pencil. Keep the pencil lines light, so that they will not be visible later. Using a metal ruler and a scalpel, lightly score along the pencil lines. The scored lines will help you achieve crisp edges when applying the paint or stain.

6

TRADE SECRETS

- *Brushing off the liming paste will produce copious amounts of dust, so work outside if possible. If you have to work inside, cover the surrounding area with dust sheets. When finished, immediately remove and vacuum the dust sheets to avoid spreading dust around the house.*

- *Use acrylic varnish only: an oil-based varnish will yellow over time and spoil the limed effect.*

- *A similar look can be achieved without the use of liming paste. Follow Steps 1–4, then tint matt acrylic varnish using three drops of white universal tinter and apply to the door instead of liming paste.*

6 • REMOVING THE LIMING PASTE

Wear a dust mask at this stage, to avoid inhaling any dust. Using a small, soft wire brush, gently brush away the paste, working in the direction of the grain. Brush the excess dust off with a dusting brush, or vacuum it away, then go back over it with a slightly damp cloth to remove all remaining dust.

7 • SEALING

The marquetry-style design will now have a beautiful pastel-like, silvery appearance. Use a varnish brush to carefully apply an even coat of white polish shellac to the entire door, taking care not to dislodge the liming paste in the grain.

8 • FINISHING

Varnish with three coats of matt acrylic varnish, allowing each coat to dry thoroughly before applying the next.

7

FURNITURE

A wooden knob painted and limed to match the door lends a sense of continuity to this soft, rich effect.

Shades of scarlet

Here we see how reds can be used to create a wide range of effects, each with its own unique ambience. From the beauty of woodgraining in rich cherry tones to funky colourwashed checks in red and orange, and from a luxurious red-and-black tortoiseshell design to simple Chinese red lacquer-style, it is possible to achieve a sense of drama, cheerfulness or elegance with the red palette.

▲ FANTASY WOODGRAIN

A faux woodgrain that imitates burr walnut. After priming (see pages 6-9), apply two coats of light terracotta matt emulsion or wood paint and seal with white polish shellac. Mix up a chestnut-brown vinegar glaze to the consistency of milk using burnt sienna and burnt umber pigments (see Step 2, page 112). Brush the glaze onto the inner panel (see Step 3, page 113), then roll a sausage-shaped piece of Plasticine over it to create a regular pattern. Dab a damp sea sponge over the pattern to reveal some base colour; soften with a badger-hair softener. Repeat on the outer panel. When dry, carefully glide on a coat of button polish shellac (or raw umber-tinted white polish shellac). Do not brush over any area twice. When dry, shellac again, then apply three coats of eggshell acrylic varnish. *Suitable for all surfaces.*

◀ FRUIT DECOUPAGE

A fruit decoupage design makes a classic, stylish statement. After priming (see pages 6-9), apply two coats of cream matt emulsion or wood paint. Seal fruit decoupage motifs with button polish shellac; cut out when dry. Stick each motif onto the inner panel using diluted PVA glue (see Step 5, page 39). Seal with white polish shellac. Paint bright red matt emulsion on the inside rim of the panel and on the outer edges of the door. When dry, varnish with two coats of matt acrylic varnish tinted with two drops of raw umber. *Suitable for all surfaces.*

▲ CHERRY STENCIL ON SPATTER

A simple fruit stencil on a subtle veil of spattered colour produces this lively effect. After priming (see pages 6-9), apply two coats of coffee-cream matt emulsion or wood paint. Mask off the outer panel. Mix up a light terracotta glaze to the consistency of milk (see Scumble glaze effects, page 19) and brush onto the inner panel; stipple (see Scumble glaze effects, page 19). Add 10ml (2 tsp) of water and two drops of burnt sienna and yellow ochre universal tinters to the glaze and spatter the inner panel (see Step 6, page 95). Add two more drops of burnt sienna and three drops of red and spatter again. Finally, spatter with diluted coffee-cream paint. Use a simple fruit motif and stencil with red and green stencil paint. Hand-paint dark green veins onto the leaves. Paint the inner rim of the inside panel red. Remove the tape. Leave to dry overnight, then apply three coats of matt acrylic varnish.
Suitable for all surfaces.

▼ RED COLOURWASH CHECK

Red and orange checks make a bold, funky statement. After priming (see pages 6-9), apply two coats of cream non-absorbent matt emulsion or matt emulsion sealed with matt acrylic varnish. Stick horizontal rows of low-tack masking tape at 100mm (4 in) and 25mm (1 in) intervals. Mix a red colourwash and wash over the door; soften with a hog-hair softener (see Colourwashing, page 18). With a slightly damp sea sponge, wipe away the colourwash from the narrow stripes. Drag a bright yellow colourwash over the narrow stripes (see Scumble glaze effects, page 19). When dry, stick vertical rows of low-tack masking tape at the same intervals and repeat the colourwashing process. Remove the tape. After 24 hours, apply three coats of eggshell acrylic varnish.
Suitable for all surfaces; man-made surfaces will require more drying time.

▼ RED-BLACK TORTOISESHELL

Faux tortoiseshell creates a traditional Victorian look. After priming (see pages 6-9), apply two coats of red matt emulsion or wood paint. When dry, mask off the frame and brush untinted scumble glaze (the consistency of thick cream) onto the panels (see Scumble glaze effects, page 19). Mix three parts burnt sienna to one part black artists' acrylic paints together and hand-paint diagonal oblong shapes. Add black to the mixture and paint dark lines around the shapes. Dab a damp sea sponge over the marks to reveal the base colour; soften with a badger-hair softener. Mix two drops of crimson and burnt sienna tinters in button polish shellac and apply two coats (allow to dry between coats). Remove the tape; apply three coats of eggshell acrylic varnish. Apply gold gilding wax (see Gilding wax, page 23) or gold varnish to the moulding.
Suitable for all surfaces; most effective on small panels.

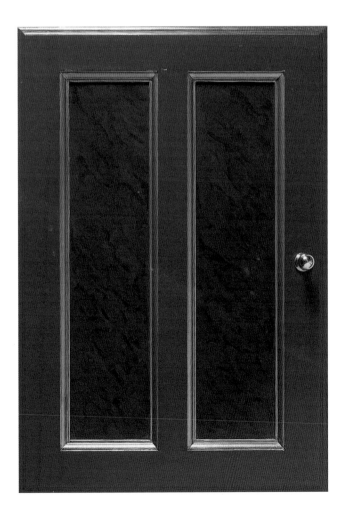

▲ MAHOGANY GRAINING AND TROMPE L'OEIL MOULDING

This faux woodgrain effect emulates rich mahogany panelling. After priming (see pages 6-9), apply a coat of terracotta vinyl silk emulsion. Mask off a frame of low-tack masking tape 70mm (3 in) in from the door's edge. Mix some scumble glaze to the consistency of single cream and colour with burnt umber and a drop of black artists' acrylics. Brush the glaze over the whole door, then hand-paint random stripes using burnt umber and black. Flog (see Step 3, page 57); soften with a badger-hair softener. Add heartgrain shapes by painting concentric horseshoe shapes in burnt amber and black, then soften again. When dry, remove the tape and mask the painted areas around the unpainted lines. Drag a nearly-black glaze over the unpainted stripes (see Scumble glaze effects, page 19). When dry, retape and paint a brown line down the centre of each stripe. Remove the tape. Seal with button polish shellac. When dry, varnish with three coats of eggshell acrylic varnish.
Suitable for all surfaces; most effective on a flat door.

▼ BRIGHT LACQUER

The glossy effect of traditional lacquer is recreated in a
contemporary style. Apply two coats of primer tinted red (see
pages 6-9), sanding between coats, then apply two coats of
bright red matt emulsion or wood paint; sand between coats
once again. When dry, apply white polish shellac as smoothly
as possible. After 24 hours, apply a second coat. More coats of
shellac can be added for a deeper lustre and sheen if desired.
Always allow the shellac to dry for 24 hours between coats.
Apply three coats of gloss acrylic varnish.
Suitable for all surfaces; most effective on a flat or Shaker-style door.

▲ HAND-PAINTED STRIPES AND DISTRESSED PAINTWORK

This technique creates a fun, contemporary feel – try it in
bold shades, or in muted, subtle tones (see Choosing colours,
pages 24-27, for guidance). After priming (see pages 6-9),
apply two coats of cream matt emulsion or wood paint. Mask
off the outer panel and select five shades of wood paint.
Starting on the left, hand-paint stripes down the length of the
panel using a 5mm (¼ in) one-stroke brush. Repeat the colours
in the same order across the panel. Go over the stripes twice to
ensure coverage. When dry, apply a coat of matt acrylic
varnish. Remove the tape and mask off the inner panel. Rub
candle wax onto the frame, then paint the frame and inside rim
with two coats of red matt emulsion; when dry, distress with
medium-grade wire wool (see Distressing, page 18). Varnish
with three coats of matt acrylic varnish.
Suitable for wooden surfaces.

BLUES & GREENS

RELAXING, HARMONIOUS AND PEACEFUL ARE WORDS THAT ARE COMMONLY USED TO DESCRIBE THE BLUE AND GREEN PALETTE. TYPICALLY ASSOCIATED WITH THE NATURAL WORLD, BLUES AND GREENS REMIND US OF BLUE SKIES, SPRING LEAVES, RIVERS AND OCEANS — THE PLACES WE VISIT TO UNWIND AND RELAX. ON ITS OWN, BLUE IS A CONTEMPLATIVE, RESTFUL COLOUR, WHILE GREEN IS SOMEWHAT MORE VIGOROUS, YET REGENERATIVE AND BALANCED. WHEN PAIRED TOGETHER, THE RESULT IS AN AMBIENCE THAT IS RESTFUL, SOOTHING AND HARMONIOUS. BOTH OF THESE COLOURS LEND THEMSELVES TO A WIDE VARIETY OF FINISHES, AND ARE INHERENTLY WELL SUITED TO TRADITIONAL AS WELL AS CONTEMPORARY STYLES. AS RECEDING COLOURS, BLUES AND GREENS ARE OFTEN USED AS PART OF A PATTERN, USUALLY IN COMBINATION WITH WHITE; THEY ARE ALSO EFFECTIVE WHEN USED ALONE, AS PLAIN, FLAT COLOURS. IN ROOMS WHERE COOLER SHADES OF BLUE OR GREEN FEATURE PROMINENTLY, ACCENTS OF RED, ORANGE OR YELLOW CAN BE ADDED FOR A SENSE OF WARMTH.

Gingham *checks*

USING SCUMBLE GLAZE EFFECTS to emulate different types of textiles and textures is a popular and fashionable design source for interiors. Here we pick up on this trend, using acrylic scumble glaze to create a wonderful gingham texture. Ideal for adding charm and character to cottage- or Shaker-style kitchens, this paint finish can be used throughout your kitchen, or on occasional units only — paint the remaining units in the same two shades used to make the checks. Based on dragging using a specialist long-bristled brush, the actual paint technique used to create this finish is very simple. All you need is a little time and patience — and plenty of lining tape!

MATERIALS AND EQUIPMENT

UNIVERSAL TINTERS: GREEN, RAW UMBER
IVORY HIGHLY PIGMENTED WOOD PAINT
2 DECORATORS' PAINTBRUSHES
2 VARNISH BRUSHES, ONE IN A SMALLER SIZE
SMALL DRAGGING BRUSH
ARTISTS' SABLE BRUSH
10MM (⅜ IN) LOW-TACK LINING TAPE
PLASTIC RULER
PENCIL
SET-SQUARE OR SPIRIT LEVEL
PLASTIC DRAWING RUBBER
PAINT KETTLE
FINE-GRADE SANDPAPER
ACRYLIC SCUMBLE GLAZE
ACRYLIC EGGSHELL VARNISH

1 • PREPARATION

Prepare a solid wood or MDF surface following the instructions on pages 6-9. Apply two coats of ivory wood paint, sanding in between coats using fine-grade sandpaper. When dry, apply a coat of acrylic eggshell varnish with a varnish brush. Allow to dry fully.

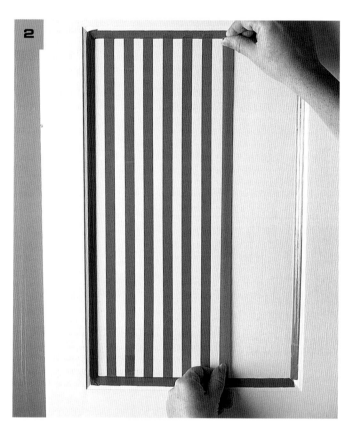

2 • TAPING THE FIRST LINES

Use low-tack lining tape to mask the moulding between the inner and outer panels. Start applying the tape in vertical lines on the inner panel. The gap between lines should be the same thickness as the tape — use a ruler for complete accuracy. Draw a line around the centre of the outer panel; fix the tape centrally over the line.

3 • MIXING THE GLAZE

Pour two parts acrylic scumble glaze into a paint kettle, and make up the final third with equal parts of water and acrylic eggshell varnish. Add four or five drops of green universal tinter, then tone down slightly with a drop of raw umber. Stir well.

4 • DRAGGING THE GLAZE

Using a small varnish brush, brush the glaze onto the inner panel of the door, making sure that an even coverage is achieved. Take a small dragging brush and drag it down the door through the glaze, repeating this movement until you have achieved an even set of dragged lines through the still-wet glaze. Glaze and drag the outer panel of the door as well, brushing downwards on the vertical and across on the horizontal. Allow to dry for 30 minutes.

5 • REMOVING THE TAPE

When the glaze begins to harden, peel off all of the tape lines, with the exception of those masking the moulding (this will be left ivory). Allow to dry for two full hours, or until the glaze has completely hardened.

6 • TAPING THE SECOND LINES

Fix lines of tape at right-angles to the first lines — use a set-square or spirit level for guidance if you like. Once again, the gap between the lines should be the same thickness as the tape. Place a piece of tape continuing the line of the moulding at each end of the door frame, creating a right-angle square in each corner. Make a smaller right angle at the corner, lining the tape up with the previous line. The corner lines should now show two concentric right-angles (see above inset).

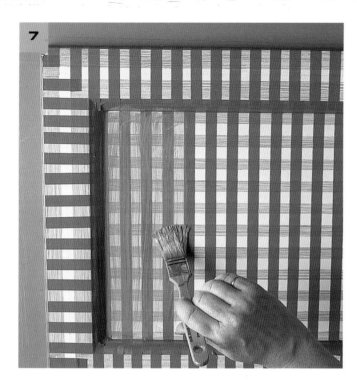

7 • DRAGGING THE SECOND GLAZE

Apply an even coat of glaze to the inner panel with the smaller varnish brush. Take the small dragging brush and drag it horizontally across the door — if the door is off its hinges, turn it so that you can drag in a downward motion — until you have evenly dragged lines. Leave the glaze to dry until it starts to harden, then remove the tape, including those strips covering the moulding.

8 • PAINTING IN DETAIL

To create an effective gingham-style border, take up some of the glaze on an artists' sable brush, and paint small strokes imitating a backstitch down the centre of the ivory line left on the outer panel. Allow to dry for 24 hours, or until fully dry.

FURNITURE

A plain white ceramic or enamel knob or a simple chrome handle would be a perfect finishing touch for this charming design.

9 • FINISHING

Rub out the pencil lines on the outer panel and brush or vacuum away the rubber dust. Apply three coats of acrylic eggshell varnish, allowing each coat to dry thoroughly before applying the next.

Duck-egg *speckle*

2

Based on the established paint technique of spattering, the subtle veil of speckled colour created by this effect is often used to imitate the look of natural stones and precious minerals such as sandstone, porphyry, granite and lapis lazuli. Here we use this technique to produce a slightly different, more delicate effect, recreating the look of a duck-egg shell in blues and greys.

A very simple technique, spattering relies upon the subtlety of similar tones and hues spattered finely onto a pale, stippled background. Ideally applied to plain, flat cupboard doors or large panelled doors, this effect is perfect for a room that needs a slight lift, but not necessarily a radical transformation.

MATERIALS AND EQUIPMENT
Pale blue matt emulsion
Artists' acrylic paints: green, blue, black, raw umber, white
2 decorators' paintbrushes
Varnish brush
5 fitch brushes or stencil brushes
Paint kettle
Low-tack masking tape
Stippling block
Paint mixing palette or saucers
Step ladder (optional)
Fine-grade sandpaper (for a wooden or MDF door)
Acrylic scumble glaze
Matt acrylic varnish

1 • PREPARATION
Prepare a solid wood, MDF, melamine, vinyl or laminate surface following the instructions on pages 6-9, laying on two coats of primer. Apply two coats of pale blue matt emulsion, allowing the first coat to dry thoroughly before applying the second. Sand between coats using fine-grade sandpaper on wooden and MDF doors. Allow a full 24 hours for the paint to dry. Using a varnish brush, apply a coat of matt acrylic varnish, and allow to dry thoroughly.

2 • MIXING THE GLAZE
Make up a glaze in a paint kettle as follows: add a bit of blue and green artists' acrylic paint to a mixture of two-thirds acrylic scumble glaze to one-third equal amounts of matt acrylic varnish and water. (The varnish is used here to hasten the drying time of the glaze).

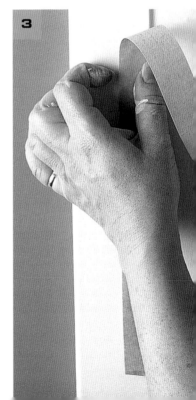

3

3 • MASKING THE PANEL
Using low-tack masking tape, mask off the entire outer panel, leaving the inner panel clear.

4 • STIPPLING THE GLAZE

Using a decorators' paintbrush, apply a coat of glaze to the door panel in uneven, loose brushstrokes. Take the stippling block and, using a 'pouncing' motion, work it into the still-wet glaze. Continue stippling, wiping any excess glaze off the block as you work, until a soft veil of glaze covers the entire panel. Set aside for approximately 30 minutes, or until the glaze starts to harden.

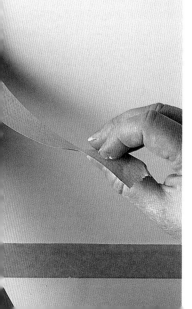

5 • MIXING COLOURS

Mix up five different colours of artists' acrylic paints as follows: create an off-white by mixing a dab of raw umber with white; a pale turquoise using white and a bit of blue and green; a mid-tone turquoise using white, blue and a dab of green; a mid-tone grey using white, black and a dab of raw umber; and a darker grey using white, black and a dab of raw umber. Add water to each of the colours, until all are the consistency of single cream.

6 • SPATTERING

Spatter using each of the five colours, as follows: dip a dry fitch or stencil brush into the paint, and position it directly in front of or above the area to be spattered. Holding the brush in one hand, flick it down over the forefinger of your other hand. Spatter first with the pale turquoise, covering the entire area with a fine spray. Next, spatter the darker turquoise, the mid-tone grey, the dark grey, and finally, the white. Allow to dry for a full 24 hours.

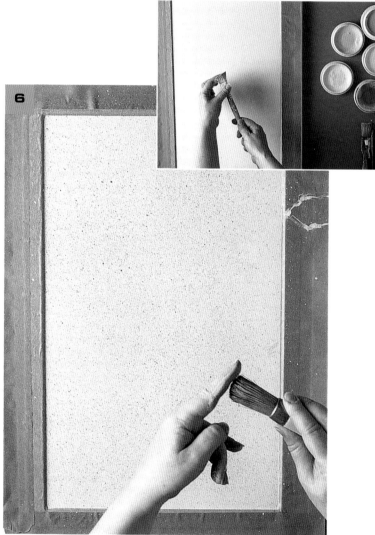

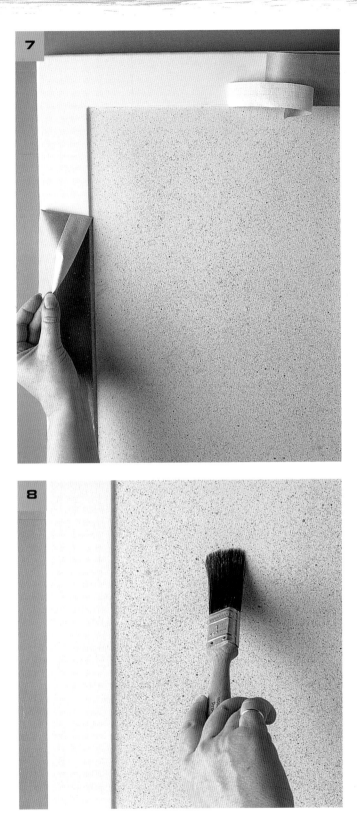

7 • REMOVING THE TAPE

When the spattered paint has fully dried, remove the masking tape by gently peeling it back upon itself.

TRADE SECRETS

- *For this technique to work properly, it is important that the paint is the right consistency. If the paint drips before you begin spattering, this means that it is too thin; if the paint comes off the brush in large droplets during spattering, dilute it with more water.*

- *It is best to remove the door so that you can spatter while standing above it, ensuring an even distribution of spatter marks. If removal is impossible, use a step ladder to position yourself level with the surface while spattering. This will help prevent the spattered paint from becoming overly dense at the bottom.*

8 • FINISHING

When the paint is completely dry, apply three coats of matt acrylic varnish, allowing each coat to dry thoroughly before applying the next.

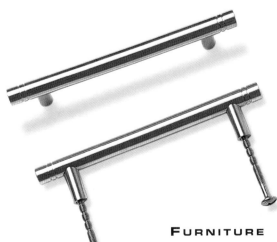

FURNITURE

Brushed chrome handles are the natural choice to illuminate the cool blue tones of this design.

Blue-and-white
Portuguese-style folk art

Blue and white is a popular colour combination, and is often prominent in crockery and ceramics. The famous Willow pattern, based on oriental chinoiserie designs, Delft tiles and ceramics from Holland, Spode china, and traditional Mediterranean pottery have all made use of this attractive pairing of colours.

Here we apply the crisp simplicity of blue and white to the kitchen, developing a design based upon an original piece of Portuguese pottery painted in a folk-art style.

MATERIALS AND EQUIPMENT

White matt emulsion
Artists' acrylic paints: cobalt blue,
ultramarine blue, white
Decorators' paintbrush
Varnish brush
Medium artists' sable brush
Fine artists' sable brush
Sharp pencil
Tracing paper
Low-tack masking tape
2 jam jars
Lint-free cloth
Fine-grade sandpaper (for a wooden or
MDF door)
Acrylic scumble glaze
Matt acrylic varnish
Blue-tinted wax polish

1 • PREPARATION

This technique lends itself to solid wood doors with central panels, but it can also be applied to melamine, laminate, vinyl and MDF doors. Prepare the surface following the instructions on pages 6-9. Apply two coats of white matt emulsion, allowing the first coat to dry before applying the second. Sand between coats using fine-grade sandpaper on wooden and MDF doors. With a varnish brush, apply one coat of matt acrylic varnish.

2 • TRACING THE DESIGN

Choose a blue-and-white ceramic design. On a piece of tracing paper, trace the main part of the design. If the design needs to be elongated in order to fit the central panel, parts of it can be repeated.

3 • TRANSFERRING THE DESIGN

Turn the tracing paper over and centre it on the door panel, holding it in place with some masking tape. Using a sharp pencil, draw over each traced line, transferring the design onto the door.

4 • DESIGNING THE BORDER

Select a detail from the original design that can be repeated as a border. Trace and transfer this design as before, around the border of the door. Alternatively, draw a border freehand, or paint a simple thin line using two lines of low-tack masking tape as a guide.

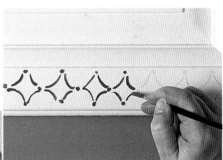

5 • MIXING THE PAINT

Mix some cobalt blue and ultramarine blue artists' acrylic paint together in two separate jam jars. Add different amounts of white artists' acrylic paint to each jar, creating a mid-tone blue and a darker shade of blue. Add a little acrylic scumble glaze and water to both mixtures until they are the consistency of single cream.

6 • PAINTING THE DESIGN

Using a medium artists' sable brush, paint in the design with the mid-toned blue; use the original design as a guide. Paint using short, rounded brushstrokes for a folk-art look. When dry, take up some dark blue on the fine artists' sable brush and paint in the shadows and details. Paint the border pattern in the same way.

7

8

7 • ADDING DECORATIVE DETAIL

Take up some of the dark blue on the fine sable brush and hold the loaded paintbrush at a slight angle to the edge of the raised panel or moulding. Run the brush along the moulding to create a thin line. Mix a pale wash by adding more water to the mid-tone blue paint, then use the medium artists' sable brush to paint this wash along the moulding. Allow to dry.

8 • FINISHING

Apply three coats of matt acrylic varnish, allowing each coat to dry thoroughly before applying the next. Take up some blue-tinted wax polish on a lint-free cloth and apply it to the edges and corners of the panel and border to create areas of soft shading.

FURNITURE

Paint a wooden knob using white wood paint, and allow to dry thoroughly. Choose a detail from your design, and copy it onto the knob using either the mid-tone or darker blue – or both – as you like.

TRADE SECRETS

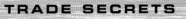

- *Use loose brushstrokes to paint in the less intricate parts of the design, holding the brush handle anywhere from the middle to the end for greater ease of movement. This will result in a 'folk-art' painting style. For the more detailed portions of the design, hold the brush handle closer to the bristles to achieve greater control.*

Ocean splendour

Blues and greens in both deep and pastel shades lend themselves to modern styles, as well as to more traditional ones – designs that combine both styles suit this palette as well. Delicate hand-painted willow leaves in muted greens, a faux lapis lazuli finish, stylish polished plaster squares in aqua hues and distressing in rich blue and pale green are just a few examples of how this colour palette can be used to gorgeous effect.

▲ HAND-PAINTED WILLOW

A delicate willow design in muted greens creates a sense of calm. Prime (see pages 6-9), then apply two coats of pale green non-absorbent matt emulsion or matt emulsion sealed with matt acrylic varnish. Mix a pale green colourwash (see Colourwashing, page 18) and wash over the door. Leave overnight, then seal with matt acrylic varnish. Transfer a willow design to the door (see Step 6, page 36). Paint the leaves using two tones of green and the twigs using brown. Mask a border with low-tack masking tape; paint in green to the near edges of the willow design (see photo). Remove the tape. Apply three coats of matt acrylic varnish.
Suitable for all surfaces.

◀ DISTRESSING, STENCILLING AND WAXING

A charming Provençal-style design. After priming (see pages 6-9), apply two coats of blue matt emulsion or wood paint. Rub on some candle wax. Apply two coats of pale green matt emulsion or wood paint. When dry, distress with medium-grade wire wool (see Distressing, page 18). Using a linear stencil and a slightly darker green, stencil the upright panels. When dry, apply three coats of matt acrylic varnish. Highlight the moulding and stencilling with gold gilding wax (see Gilding wax, page 23).
Suitable for all surfaces.

▼ DISTRESSED PAINT AND EMBROIDERY SAMPLER EFFECT

An embroidery sampler is set off against distressed paintwork for a folk look. After priming (see pages 6-9), apply two coats of pale grey matt emulsion or wood paint. Rub on some candle wax, then paint with two coats of pale green matt emulsion or wood paint. When dry, distress with medium-grade wire wool (see Distressing, page 18). Seal a colour photocopy of an embroidery sampler with white polish shellac (see Step 2, page 38); when dry, cut to fit the door panel. Stick this down using diluted PVA glue, laying the top down first, then smoothing the whole picture down. When dry, seal with white polish shellac. Allow to dry completely, then apply three coats of matt acrylic varnish.

Suitable for wooden and MDF surfaces.

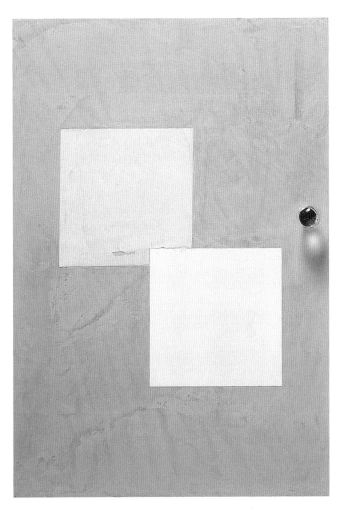

▲ POLISHED PLASTER SQUARES

A stylish, modern design using polished plaster in three tones. Apply two coats of primer tinted green (see pages 6-9). Mix up aquamarine, white and pale aqua (aquamarine mixed with the white) batches of polished plaster (see Step 2, page 76). Apply a fine layer of the aquamarine, remove the excess, and smooth out (see Step 3, page 77). When dry, apply a second coat; when nearly dry, polish to a sheen (see Step 4, page 77). Mark up two overlapping squares. Stick low-tack masking tape around the lower square. Apply two thin coats of pale aqua plaster to the masked square and polish. When dry, remove the tape. Tape up the overlapping square and repeat the process with the white plaster. Polish the entire surface when dry. Seal with gloss acrylic varnish or liquid wax (see Liquid waxes, page 23).

Suitable for flat wooden and MDF surfaces.

▼ HAND-PAINTED STRIPES

Cool blue and green stripes make a bold statement. After priming (see pages 6-9), apply two coats of pale turquoise matt emulsion or wood paint. When dry, stick two rows of low-tack masking tape around the door's frame. Select four shades of blue and green matt emulsion or wood paint (see Choosing colours, pages 24-27, for guidance). Paint freehand stripes using different brushes to create different stripe widths. Don't worry if the stripes wobble – it's all part of the look. When dry, remove the tapes. Apply three coats of eggshell acrylic varnish.

Suitable for all surfaces.

▲ BLUE COLOURWASH WITH GOLD STENCIL

Rich blue with sophisticated gold stencilling adds a splash of colour to the kitchen. After priming (see pages 6-9), apply two coats of pale turquoise non-absorbent matt emulsion or matt emulsion sealed with matt acrylic varnish. Mix a cobalt blue colourwash and wash over the door (see Colourwashing, page 18). After 24 hours, seal with matt acrylic varnish. Apply a second coat of colourwash to the central panel. Stencil gold stencil paint through a linear border stencil on the vertical outer panels. Leave to dry, then varnish with three coats of matt or eggshell acrylic varnish.

Suitable for all surfaces.

▼ LAPIS LAZULI EFFECT

Lapis lazuli with gold distressing creates a sumptuous feel. Prime, (see pages 6-9) then apply two coats of turquoise matt emulsion or wood paint (sand between coats). Mix an ultramarine glaze and a Prussian blue glaze (see Scumble glaze effects, page 19) to the consistency of single cream. Mask off the outer panel. Using two sea sponges, dab both colours onto the inner panel, leaving some base colour showing. Leave for 10 minutes and repeat; repeat a third time. Paint tiny dots of gilding size randomly across the surface; dab on gold metallic powder. After 10 minutes, brush off the excess. Seal the gold dots with white polish shellac. When dry, remove the tape from the frame, rub on candle wax, and cover with gold paint. Distress with medium-grade wire wool (see Distressing, page 18) when dry. Apply three coats of eggshell acrylic varnish. *Suitable for wooden and MDF surfaces.*

▲ WOVEN DENIM EFFECT

The simple appeal of denim is used here to stylish effect. After priming (see pages 6-9), mask off the outer panel. Apply two coats of pale blue matt emulsion or wood paint to the inner panel. Seal with matt acrylic varnish. Mix up a glaze using ⅔ matt acrylic varnish and ⅓ water to the consistency of single cream and tint with blue, raw umber and a little white (see Scumble glaze effects, page 19). Brush the glaze vertically and evenly onto the inner panel, then drag a dragging brush repeatedly through the glaze until an even effect is achieved (see Dragging, page 19). After 15 minutes, repeat the dragging process horizontally. When dry, varnish with matt acrylic varnish. Mask off the inner panel. Paint the outer panel and edges with two coats of sea blue matt emulsion or wood paint. When dry, apply three coats of matt acrylic varnish. *Suitable for all door surfaces.*

BLACK, WHITE & GREY

Whether used alone or in combination, black, white and grey are typically associated with a sleek, modern style. Black on its own should be used sparingly, as it absorbs light. For a reflective quality,

a black surface can be finished with gloss or metallic varnish. Black can also be lightened to a charcoal shade for a softer, more subtle effect. When paired with white — or with virtually any other colour — black becomes an elegant accent. The opposite of black, white has long been a decorative favourite. Today, it is usually associated with the minimalist look. The most reflective of colours, white harmonizes with all other colours, whether bright or neutral. Paired with black, it provides a clear, bold contrast; paired with grey, it lends an air of tranquillity and sophistication. Grey can be bland on its own, but the addition of deeper and lighter tones will result in a balanced colour scheme. The addition of metallic fittings and accessories enhances the look of all three colours.

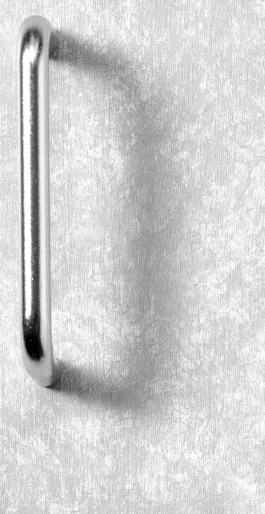

Grey *rag-rolling*

WHEN THE PAINT effects revolution ignited in the 1980s, rag-rolling was among the most widely used techniques. Its popularity remains, but a softer, more gentle approach is now favoured. Today, the use of subtle, close colour combinations lends an understated, contemporary twist to this finish.

There are two ways to apply the rag-rolling technique – the first uses the rag to roll the glaze on, and the second involves painting a glaze first, and then rag-rolling it off. Here we apply the first version of this technique. Rolling three tones of grey onto a white surface, we emulate the character and colour of pale Carrara marble to create a cool, serene kitchen setting.

MATERIALS AND EQUIPMENT

WHITE VINYL SILK EMULSION
IVORY HIGHLY PIGMENTED WOOD PAINT
SOFT BLACK HIGHLY PIGMENTED WOOD PAINT
DECORATORS' PAINTBRUSH
BADGER-HAIR SOFTENER
ARTISTS' SABLE BRUSH
VARNISH BRUSH
4 PAINT KETTLES
LOW-TACK MASKING TAPE
LARGE COTTON CLOTH
FINE-GRADE SANDPAPER
ACRYLIC SCUMBLE GLAZE
MATT ACRYLIC VARNISH
ACRYLIC EGGSHELL VARNISH (OPTIONAL)

1 • PREPARATION

This technique is best suited to solid wood and MDF doors – it is not appropriate for melamine, vinyl or laminate doors. Prepare the surface following the instructions on pages 6-9. Apply two coats of white vinyl silk emulsion, allowing the first coat to dry thoroughly before applying the second. Sand between coats using fine-grade sandpaper.

2 • MIXING THE GLAZES

Create three coloured glazes as follows: in three separate paint kettles, mix ivory and soft black wood paints to produce three tones of grey: pale, mid-tone, and darker. Add one-third acrylic scumble glaze and one-third equal amounts of matt acrylic varnish and water to each kettle.

3 • RAG-ROLLING THE FIRST GLAZE

Use low-tack masking tape to mask off the door's outer panel. Cut a large cotton cloth into three pieces. Partially dip one piece of cloth into the mid-tone grey glaze, taking care not to saturate it. Work the glaze through the cloth, until the entire cloth has absorbed some of the glaze. Roll the cloth into a sausage shape, then lay it on the bottom left-hand corner of the door's inner panel. Using arcing movements, roll the cloth up the panel, repeating until the entire surface is evenly covered with ragging marks. Use a new rag when necessary.

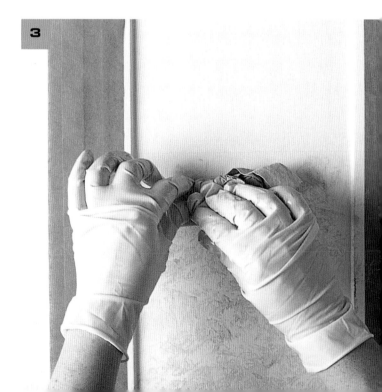

4

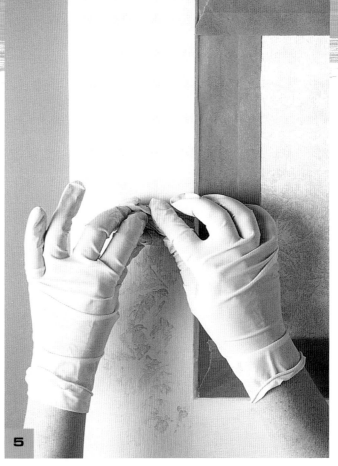

5

4 • SOFTENING THE GLAZE

To soften and blend the effect of the rag-rolling, lightly dust a badger-hair softener over the still-wet glaze in all directions. Leave until thoroughly dry.

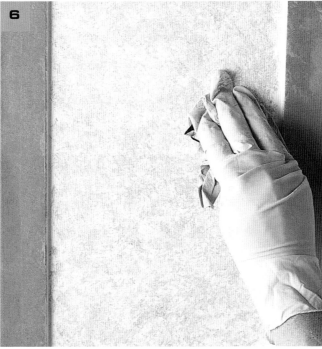

6

5 • RAG-ROLLING THE SECOND GLAZE

Remove the masking tape from the outer panel and mask off the inner panel. Using a new rag, repeat the rag-rolling process on the outer panel, this time using the pale grey glaze. Once again, dust lightly with the softener, blending any hard edges or distinct marks. Leave for five minutes, then lightly rag on a touch of the mid-tone grey glaze. Blend once again with the softener, and allow to dry fully.

6 • RAG-ROLLING THE THIRD GLAZE

Remove the masking tape from the inner panel, and mask off the outer panel once again. Using a new rag, take up the darker grey glaze and lightly roll it over the inner panel. Again, blend using the softener. Remove the tape from the outer panel, and check that the glaze has been evenly distributed over both the inner and outer panels; dab extra glaze onto any uneven patches. Soften once more, then allow to dry thoroughly.

7

7 • PAINTING IN DETAIL

Mask off the outer panel once again, so that the tape borders the inner panel. Mix a little ivory with some soft black wood paint in a paint kettle to create a charcoal grey; add some water to thin out the paint. Using an artists' sable brush, paint the rim between the inner and outer panels. Paint an equally thin line along the very edge of the outer panel as well. Allow to dry thoroughly.

8 • FINISHING

Apply three coats of either matt or acrylic eggshell varnish, allowing each coat to dry thoroughly before applying the next. Do not use oil-based varnish, as this will yellow over time.

8

TRADE SECRETS

- *Do not overload the rag with glaze — if it is dripping or sodden, this means that it is oversaturated, and a new rag should be used for best effect.*

- *Always roll in arced lines rather than straight lines, so that the ragging marks are irregular. Rescrunching the cloth periodically will ensure that the same markings are not repeated.*

FURNITURE

Silver knobs or handles would subtly complement the various tones of grey used here.

Vinegar glaze *fingerprinting*

The tradition of vinegar glazing began in the 19th century, when craftsmen used it as a cheap and simple solution to the increasing demand for faux graining on furniture and woodwork. Although not as sophisticated as some of the more formal glazes, vinegar glaze lends itself to numerous forms of pattern-making, such as printing with corks, putty, folded cards and fingertips.

Here we work with a black glaze, making simple repetitive marks with the fingertip for a pewter chainmail effect. The look is further embellished by a graphite varnish panel, and then finished with a high-gloss varnish for a striking, contemporary feel.

1 • PREPARATION

This technique is only suitable for solid wood and MDF doors – it is unsuitable for melamine, vinyl and laminate surfaces. Prepare the surface following the instructions on pages 6-9. Apply two coats of ivory matt emulsion, letting the first coat dry before applying the second, and sanding in between coats using fine-grade sandpaper. Sand the final coat, then seal with a coat of white shellac, brushed on as evenly as possible with a varnish brush.

2 • MIXING THE GLAZE

Put 40ml (8 tsp) of black powder pigment into a paint kettle. Add a little malt vinegar and mix into a paste. When the pigment has dissolved, add 250ml (1 cup) of vinegar (this will be enough for two doors), and mix thoroughly. Add three drops of black water-based universal tinter, 10ml (2 tsp) of washing-up liquid, and 10ml (2 tsp) of sugar. Stir until fully dissolved. The glaze should now be roughly the same consistency as skimmed milk.

MATERIALS AND EQUIPMENT

IVORY MATT EMULSION
BLACK POWDER PIGMENT
BLACK UNIVERSAL TINTER
DECORATORS' PAINTBRUSH
4 VARNISH BRUSHES
MALT VINEGAR
WASHING-UP LIQUID SUGAR
PAINT KETTLE
LOW-TACK PAINTERS' TAPE
FINE-GRADE SANDPAPER
WHITE POLISH SHELLAC
READY-MADE WATER-BASED GRAPHITE VARNISH OR
METALLIC VARNISH TINTED WITH BLACK
UNIVERSAL TINTER
GLOSS ACRYLIC VARNISH

3 • APPLYING
THE GLAZE

Use low-tack masking tape to mask off the inner panel of the door. Using a varnish brush, apply a generous, even coat of glaze to the outer panel, one section at a time. Brush the coat through several times to ensure even coverage. The glaze will naturally bubble as it is applied; you'll need to brush out the larger bubbles, but the smaller ones should disappear on their own.

4 • FINGERPRINTING

Before you start fingerprinting, you may wish to experiment with the different marks made by the different points of your fingertip, and with applying different amounts of pressure. When you are ready to start fingerprinting, press the side of your third fingertip firmly down on the wet glaze, and start to print in rows, working from the inside to the outside of the border. Because each print will be slightly different, the pattern will be somewhat uneven, but this is part of the charm of this technique.

5 • GLAZING THE
INNER PANEL

Add three or four more drops of black universal tinter to the glaze. Remove the tape from the inner panel, then carefully paint with the darkened glaze. Allow to dry thoroughly.

FURNITURE
Silver or pewter handles or knobs echo the metallic look of this modern finish.

TRADE SECRETS

* *Because the ingredients of this glaze are only lightly bound together, it must always be sealed with shellac.*

* *Work in a ventilated space, as the vinegar smell can become pungent and overpowering.*

6 • SEALING
Glide a coat of white polish shellac over the entire door. Allow to dry thoroughly.

7 • VARNISHING
Lay on a coat of ready-made water-based graphite varnish or metallic varnish tinted with black universal tinter in smooth horizontal strokes, then lay it off in vertical strokes of the same direction (finish with all strokes brushing either upwards or downwards, but not both). Allow to dry, then apply a second coat in the same way. Leave until completely dry.

8 • FINISHING
Apply three even coats of gloss acrylic varnish to the entire door for a high-sheen finish, allowing each coat to dry thoroughly before applying the next.

Silver squares *on white*

2

LIGHTER AND LESS PRONOUNCED than gold, silver lends itself to minimalist fashions, especially when used together with white, ivory and pale grey. Here we introduce a quick, simple gilding technique using aluminium metal leaf – a cheaper but effective alternative to real silver leaf – on ivory with a high-gloss finish, to add a crisp and chic lift to plain painted doors. The essence of simplicity, this finish will bring an easy-to-live-with style to your kitchen. Accessorize with plenty of chrome and silver details to emphasize the contemporary feel.

MATERIALS AND EQUIPMENT
IVORY MATT EMULSION OR HIGHLY PIGMENTED
WOOD PAINT
DECORATORS' PAINTBRUSH
VARNISH BRUSH
FITCH BRUSH
13MM (½ IN) ONE-STROKE BRUSH
ALUMINIUM TRANSFER METAL LEAF
METAL RULER
PENCIL
SHARP DRESSMAKING SCISSORS OR SCALPEL
ACRYLIC GILDING SIZE
FINE-GRADE SANDPAPER (FOR WOODEN OR
MDF DOORS)
WHITE POLISH SHELLAC
GLOSS ACRYLIC VARNISH

1 • PREPARATION
Prepare a solid wood, MDF, vinyl, melamine or laminate surface following the instructions on pages 6-9. Apply two coats of ivory matt emulsion or wood paint, letting the first coat dry before applying the second. Sand between coats using fine-grade sandpaper on wooden and MDF doors. When fully dry, sand the final coat until it is smooth.

2 • CUTTING THE SQUARES
Using a pencil and ruler, draw 75mm (3 in) squares onto the backing paper of the aluminium transfer metal leaf. Cut them out with sharp dressmaking scissors or a scalpel, using a metal ruler to ensure straight lines. You will need five squares per door.

3

3 • MARKING UP
This design is essentially random, so the squares should be placed irregularly. Lay the squares out on the door until you have achieved the right balance. Using a pencil and ruler, lightly draw the squares in position onto the door. Draw each square a little smaller than the transfer metal leaf, so that the pencil marks will be completely covered by the aluminium square.

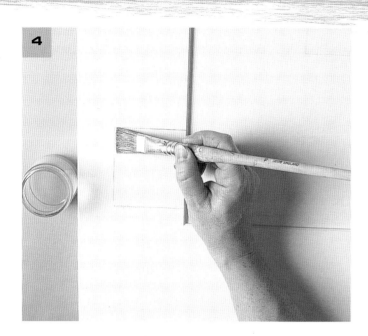

4 • SEALING THE SQUARES

Take up a little white polish shellac on a fitch brush and carefully brush it inside each drawn square. Go slightly over the lines to accommodate those aluminium squares that are a bit larger than the pencil squares. Leave until completely dry.

5 • SIZING THE SQUARES

Using a 13mm (½ in) one-stroke brush, paint acrylic gilding size onto each square, covering exactly the area of the shellac. Leave for about 15 minutes, or until the size is translucent.

6 • APPLYING THE ALUMINIUM LEAF

Position an aluminium square over a sized square, making sure it is lined up, then lay it down carefully. Smooth over the backing paper with your fingertips. Stick each square down in the same way, then smooth each one down one final time before carefully peeling off the backing paper.

7

TRADE SECRETS

- *Think about how your cupboard doors relate to each other when designing the layout of squares for each door. To plan out your design, make some paper squares and stick them onto the doors, moving them around until you achieve the right balance. The more cupboards you have, the fewer squares you will need.*

- *If your cupboards close flush, think about running a single square across two doors — to do this, just cut the square in half.*

- *Aluminium leaf works best with gloss acrylic varnish; oil-based varnish can dull its shine or cause it to yellow, making the metal appear tarnished.*

7 • SEALING
Paint over each square with white polish shellac to seal and protect the gilded areas. Allow to dry completely.

8 • FINISHING
Use a varnish brush to apply three thin, even coats of gloss acrylic varnish, allowing each coat to dry thoroughly before applying the next.

8

FURNITURE
Chrome or silver handles or knobs will complete the look of this stylish, cool, contemporary design.

Modern classics

Usually associated with a modern look, black, white and grey are actually suited to a diverse range of decorative styles. A wide variety of design possibilities is shown here, including a pewter-like liming finish, an elegant Japanese-style hand-painted design, a pastel grey combed finish and a sparkling spattered and distressed effect in grey and silver.

▼ LIMING ON BLACK

Apply liming paste over black for a pewter-like effect. Open up the grain with a firm wire brush, then apply a coat of black wood paint. When dry, apply liming paste, then rub it away using a small, soft wire brush, working in the direction of the grain (see Steps 5-6, pages 81-82). Seal with white polish shellac. When dry, apply three coats of matt acrylic varnish.
Suitable for open-grained hardwoods.

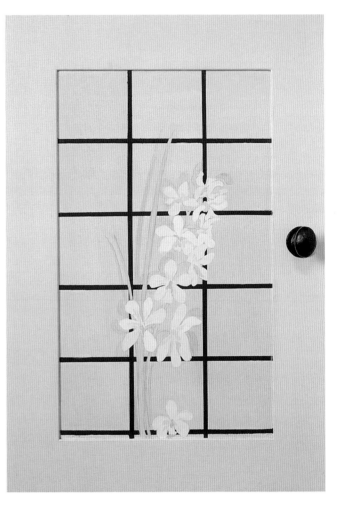

▲ JAPANESE-STYLE ORCHID DESIGN

This simple, delicate design creates a light, clean look. After priming (see pages 6-9), apply two coats of ivory matt emulsion or wood paint. Draw an orchid shape (taken from a flower book) onto tracing paper in pencil and transfer onto the inner panel (see Step 6, page 36). Tint matt acrylic varnish grey and brush onto the panel, then stipple (see Scumble glaze effects, page 19). Mark up two vertical and five horizontal lines. Stick down a double row of low-tack lining tape on the horizontal lines. Paint between the taped lines using grey artists' acrylic paint, avoiding the orchid design. Remove the tape when dry and tape up and paint between the vertical lines. When dry, paint in the orchid using white and ivory acrylic paints; use pale grey for highlights, shadows and leaves. Paint the outer panel with ivory matt emulsion tinted grey. Apply three coats of matt acrylic varnish.
Suitable for all surfaces.

▼ COOL GREY COMBING

Cool pastel grey stripes create a stylish, refined look. After priming (see pages 6-9), apply a coat of pastel grey matt emulsion or wood paint. Mask off the outer panel. Tint some combing paste to a mid-tone grey using black universal tinter (see Step 2, page 52). Brush a thick, even layer onto the inner panel and comb through with a rubber decorating comb (see Steps 3 and 4, page 53). After 24 hours, remove the tape. Touch up any uneven sections with the pastel grey paint. Use medium-grade wire wool to burnish the outer frame. Apply three coats of eggshell acrylic varnish to the frame and three coats of matt acrylic varnish to the inner panel.

Suitable for wooden and MDF surfaces.

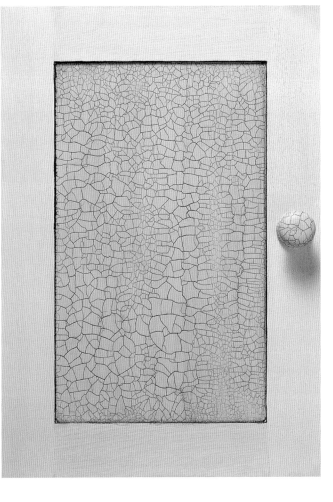

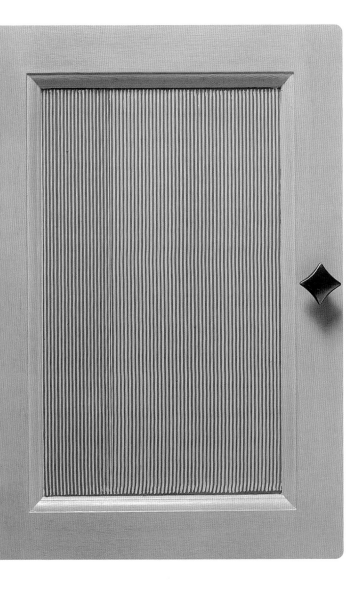

▲ OFF-WHITE WITH BLACK CRAQUELURE

Craquelure varnish is used here for a simple, classic style. After priming (see pages 6-9), apply two coats of off-white matt emulsion or wood paint. Mask off the outer panel and apply both steps of craquelure varnish to the inner panel. After a few hours, rub Payne's grey artists' oil paint into the cracks (see Step 4, page 61); remove excess oil paint with a lint-free cloth. After 24 hours, seal with white polish shellac. When dry, apply eggshell acrylic varnish. Remove the tape. Paint the rim around the inside panel with charcoal grey stencil paint. If the door is wooden, lightly sand the outer panel to reveal some of the wood grain. Seal with matt acrylic varnish.

Suitable for wooden and MDF surfaces.

▼ **HAND-PAINTED RELIEF STENCILLING**
This stencilled duck design is ideal for a waterfront home. The door does not need priming. Apply a coat of pale grey matt emulsion or wood paint. When dry, rub back with coarse-grade sandpaper to reveal the wood. Stencil ducks onto the inner panel with impasto or thick-textured paint (see Step 3, page 31). Dilute pale grey and blue-grey wood paint and paint over the dry stencil motif, painting the eyes with charcoal grey. Apply a grey wash to the moulding. When dry, use fine-grade sandpaper to gently rub the stencilling to reveal the impasto or thick-textured paint (see Step 8, page 32). Apply white wax (see Coloured wax, page 23) and buff 10 minutes later, or, near sink areas, apply matt acrylic varnish tinted white.
Suitable for wooden surfaces.

▲ **SILVER SPATTER AND DISTRESSED GILDING**
Aluminium transfer metal leaf and grey and silver spatter combine to produce this dazzling style. After priming (see pages 6-9), apply one coat of pale grey matt emulsion or wood paint. Add a drop of black and raw umber universal tinters to some of the paint and dab onto the door with a sea sponge. Mask off the moulding. Mix up a mid-tone grey glaze to the consistency of milk using ⅔ matt acrylic varnish, ⅓ water, and black and white tinters. Spatter the door (see Scumble glaze effects, page 19). Darken the glaze with a little black and spatter again. Darken again and spatter once more. Dilute the original grey paint and spatter. Finally, spatter with diluted silver paint. Allow to dry overnight, then remove the tape. Glide white polish shellac onto the moulding; when dry, gild with aluminium transfer metal leaf (see Steps 5-6, page 117). Dip medium-grade wire wool in white polish shellac and rub on the gilded areas to distress the metal leaf. When dry, apply three coats of eggshell acrylic varnish.
Suitable for wooden and MDF surfaces.

▼ SILVER CRACKLE GLAZE

A modern metallic effect. After priming (see pages 6-9), apply two coats of pale grey matt emulsion or wood paint. Mask off the outer panel and glide white polish shellac onto the inner panel. Gild aluminium transfer metal leaf to cover the whole inner panel (see Step 6, page 117) and seal with white polish shellac. When dry, vertically brush on a coat of crackle glaze. Brush the pale grey paint horizontally over the dry crackle glaze; do not brush over the same area twice. Once dry, seal with matt polyurethane varnish (see Polyurethane varnish, page 23) and allow to dry overnight. Remove the tape and paint the outer panel a very matt pale grey. When dry, apply three coats of metallic varnish (see Metallic varnishes, page 23).

Suitable for all surfaces.

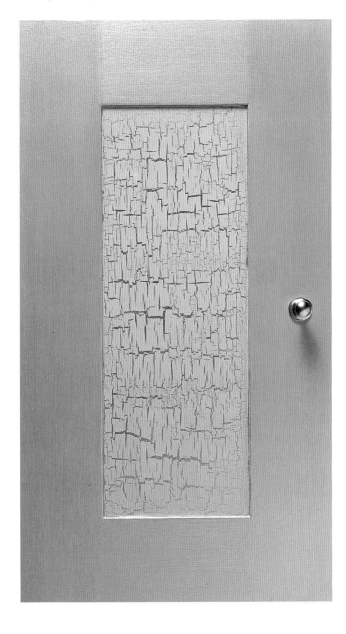

▲ SILVER STENCILLING ON BLACK

Stencil silver highlights over glossy black for an art deco style. Apply a coat of primer tinted black (see pages 6-9), followed by two coats of black matt emulsion or wood paint. Seal with white polish shellac. Select a linear stencil, spray low-tack adhesive onto the back, and lay it centrally on the outside panel. Stencil with silver stencil or wood paint. Repeat the process up the lengths of each vertical panel. Hand-paint a silver line around the inner rim of the panel. When dry, apply three coats of gloss acrylic varnish.

Suitable for all surfaces.

Resource directory

PAINTING SUPPLIES AND DECORATING TOOLS

MOST OF THE MATERIALS USED IN THIS BOOK CAN BE OBTAINED FROM LOCAL ARTISTS' SUPPLIERS OR DIY SHOPS.

ALL ABOUT ART
31 Sheen Road
Richmond, Surrey
TWI IAD
Tel: 020 8948 1277/1704
General artists' materials.

ANNIE SLOAN
Knutsford House
Park Street
Oxford OX20 IRW
Tel: 0870 601 0082
Water-based paints, varnishes and glazes. Available only through mail order.

ASKEW PAINT CENTRE
103 Askew Road
London WI2 9AS
Tel: 020 8743 6612
Paints.

ATLANTIS ART MATERIALS
146 Brick Lane
London EI 6RU
Tel: 020 7377 8855
Wide range of artists' materials, both professional and students' qualities. Mail-order service available.

J.W BOLLOM GROUP
13 Theobald's Road
London, WCIX 8FN
Tel: 020 8658 2299
Web www.bollom.com
Paints, varnishes, stains, waxes and specialist decorating equipment.

BELL CREATIVE SUPPLIES
Unit 5, Haslemere Pinnacles Estate
Coldharbour Road
Harlow, Essex CMI9 5SY
Tel: 01279 427 324
Fax: 01279 437 550
E-mail BellCS@aol.com
Wide range of art supplies.

C. BREWERS
327 Putney Bridge Road
London SWI5 2PG
Tel: 020 8788 9335
Web www.brewers.co.uk
Decorating materials and equipment.

BRODIE & MIDDLETON LTD
68 Drury Lane
London WC2B 5SP
Tel: 020 7836 3289
Decorating brushes, metallic powders, paints and pigments.

L. CORNELISSEN'S & SON LTD
105 Great Russell Street
London WCIB 3RY
Tel: 020 7636 1045
Paints, dry pigments, gilding materials and acrylic varnishes.

CRAIG & ROSE PLC
172 Leith Walk
Edinburgh EH6 5EP
Tel: 0131 554 II3I
E-mail
Inquiries@craigandrose.com
Paints and varnishes.

CROWN BERGER EUROPE LTD
P.O. Box 37
Crown House
Hollins Road, Darwen
Lancashire BB3 OBG
Tel: 0124 570 4951
Paints.

DALER-ROWNEY LTD
12 Percy Street
London WIA 2BP
Tel: 020 7636 8241
Web www.daler-rowney.com
Wide range of artists' materials.

DOVER BOOK SHOP
18 Earlham Street
London WC2H 9LN
Tel: 020 7836 2III
Web
www.thedoverbookshop.com
Decoupage sourcebooks.

FARROW & BALL LTD
Uddens Trading Estate
Wimborne
Dorset BH2I 7NL
Tel: 0120 287 6141
Web www.farrow-ball.co.uk
Period-style paints.

FOXELL & JAMES LTD
57 Farringdon Road
London ECIM 3JB
Tel: 020 7405 0152
Wood finishes, paints, acrylic varnishes and restoration products.

GREEN & STONE
259 King's Road
London SW3 5EL
Tel: 020 7352 0837
E-mail greenandstone@
enterprise.net
Pre-cut stencils, craquelure and crackle glaze varnishes, shellacs.

C. HARRISON & SON
High Street. Fordingbridge
Hants SP6 IAS
Tel: 01425 652 376
Artists' materials.

LEWIS WARD & CO.
128 Fortune Green Road
London NW6 IDN
Tel: 020 7794 3130
Specialist brushes.

LEYLAND PAINT
Kaim Decorative Products
Haddersfield Road
Birstall, Batley
West Yorkshire WFI7 9XA
Tel: 01924 354 400
Varnishes, glazes, specialist brushes.

LIBERON WAXES LTD.
Mountfield Industrial Estate
Learoyd Road
New Romney
Kent TN28 8XU
Tel: 0179 736 7555
Shellac, waxes and metallic creams.

JOHN MYLAND
80 Norwood High Street
London SE27 9NW
Tel: 020 8670 9161
Web www.mylands.co.uk
Brushes, coloured waxes, pigments, glazes and shellacs.

JOHN OLIVER LTD
33 Pembridge Road
London W11 3HG
Tel: 020 7221 6466
Paints.

PAINT MAGIC LTD
48 Golborne Road
London W10 5PR
Tel: 020 8960 9960
Fax: 020 8960 9965
Emulsions, woodpaints, colourwash, acrylic scumble, impasto, combing paste, Marmorino, polished plaster, universal tinters, crackle glaze, craquelure varnish, acrylic varnishes, liming paste, coloured waxes, gilding materials, stencils, specialist brushes and tools. Mail order service available.

PAPERS & PAINTS
4 Park Walk
London SW10 0AD
Tel: 020 7352 8626
Specialist paints and decorating materials.

PLANET PAINT
Web www.planetpaint.com
Emulsions, colourwash, wood paints, acrylic scumble glaze, universal tinters, acrylic varnishes.

E. PLOTON LTD
273 Archway Road
London N6 5AA
Tel: 020 8348 2838
Specialist decorating materials, brushes, gilding equipment and varnishes.

POLYVINT
Vint House
Rockhampton, Berkley
Gloucestershire GL13 AOT
Tel: 01454 261 276
Manufacturer of scumble glazes and paint pigments.

J H RATCLIFFE & CO
(PAINTS) LTD
135a Linaker Road
Southport PR8 5DF
Tel: 0170 453 7999
Paints and varnishes.

SIMPSONS PAINTS LTD
122-124 Broadley Street
London NW8 8BB
Tel: 020 7723 6657
Specialist brushes, gold leaf and oil glazes.

STENCIL CRAFT
115 Boldmere Rd.
Boldmere,
Sutton Coldfield
B73 5TU
Tel: 0121 354 7070
Web www.stencil.co.uk
Assorted stencils.

STUART R. STEVENSON
68 Clerkenwell Road
London EC1M 5QA
Tel: 020 7253 1693
Gilding materials.

THE STENCIL LIBRARY
Stocksfield Hall
Stocksfield, Northumberland
NE43 7TN
Tel: 01661 944944
E-mail sales@stencil-library.com
Wide range of pre-cut stencils; decoupage materials. Mail order service available.

CUPBOARD DOOR SUPPLIERS

PWS DISTRIBUTORS LTD.
P.O. Box 20
Station Road, Aycliffe
Industrial Park
Newton Aycliffe, Co.
Durham
DL5 6XJ
Tel: 1325 50 55 55
Fax: 1325 50 55 00
Web www.pws.co.uk

DOOR FURNITURE SUPPLIERS

FRANCHI LOCKS & TOOLS
278 Holloway Road
London N7 6NE
Tel: 020 7607 2200
OR

144-146 Kentish Town
Road
London NW1 9QB
Tel: 020 7267 3138
A wide variety of door furniture, plus paints and tools.

HOUSE OF BRASS
45-47 Milton Street
Nottingham, NG1 3EZ
Tel: 0115 947 5430
Web www.houseofbrass.co.uk
Period brass door furniture.

LOCKS & HANDLES
Architectural Components
Ltd
4-8 Exhibition Road,
South Kensington
London SW7 2HF
Tel: 0107 581 2401
Fax: 0107 589 4928
E-mail sales@locks-and-handles.co.uk
A wide variety of door knobs and handles.

NULINE
317 Westbourne Park Road
London W11 1EF
Tel: 020 7727 7748
A wide variety of door knobs and handles.

PWS DISTRIBUTORS LTD.
(see cupboard door suppliers, left)
A wide variety of door knobs and handles.

Index

Credits

The author and Quarto would like to thank Paint Magic Ltd for all of the wonderful paint supplies, and PWS Distributors Ltd for contributing the cupboard doors. We are also grateful to the following door hardware companies for lending knobs and handles for photography: House of Brass (0115 947 5430), Locks & Handles, Architectural Components Ltd (010 7581 2401), and PWS Distributors Ltd (01325 50 55 55).

Author acknowledgements
My thanks to Steffanie Diamond Brown and Sally Bond, and to the rest of the Quarto team, who worked with complete enthusiasm, drive and commitment throughout the project. Thanks also to Paul Forrester for many, many patient hours behind the camera, and to Katharyn Quinn and Zoe Miller for their help in priming and organizing the painted cupboard doors.

Collage extracts from Mrs. Beeton's Book of Household Management have been reproduced by kind permission of Wardlock Publishing. Decoupage motifs and stencils have been reproduced by kind permission of The Stencil Library.

Quarto would like to acknowledge.and thank the following for supplying pictures reproduced in this book:

(key: l left, r right, c centre, t top, b bottom)

p26tr Mark Wilkinson Furniture Limited, bl The Artisan Kitchen and Furniture by John Lewis of Hungerford, p27br Roundhouse Design, p42 Paula Rosa, p43br Mark Wilkinson Furniture Limited, p46 Scottwood of Nottingham, p47b Simon Taylor Furniture, p70 Chalon UK Limited, p71tr Creative Decorating, p88 Mark Wilkinson Furniture Limited, p89br Mark Wilkinson Furniture Limited, p106 Mark Wilkinson Furniture Limited, p107bl Regency Kitchens

All other photographs and illustrations are the copyright of Quarto.

While every effort has been made to credit contributors, Quarto would like to apologize should there have been any omissions or errors.